The
Nicene Creed
ILLUMINED BY MODERN THOUGHT

BY

GEDDES MACGREGOR

Grand Rapids
WILLIAM B. EERDMANS PUBLISHING COMPANY

Other Books by Geddes MacGregor

REINCARNATION AS A CHRISTIAN HOPE
SCOTLAND FOREVER HOME
GNOSIS
REINCARNATION IN CHRISTIANITY
HE WHO LETS US BE
THE RHYTHM OF GOD
PHILOSOPHICAL ISSUES IN RELIGIOUS THOUGHT
SO HELP ME GOD
A LITERARY HISTORY OF THE BIBLE
THE SENSE OF ABSENCE
GOD BEYOND DOUBT
THE HEMLOCK AND THE CROSS
THE COMING REFORMATION
INTRODUCTION TO RELIGIOUS PHILOSOPHY
THE BIBLE IN THE MAKING
CORPUS CHRISTI
THE THUNDERING SCOT
THE VATICAN REVOLUTION
THE TICHBORNE IMPOSTOR
FROM A CHRISTIAN GHETTO
LES FRONTIÈRES DE LA MORALE ET DE LA RELIGION
CHRISTIAN DOUBT
AESTHETIC EXPERIENCE IN RELIGION

Copyright © 1980 by Wm. B. Eerdmans Publishing Co.
255 Jefferson Ave. S.E., Grand Rapids, Mich. 49503

Library of Congress Cataloging in Publication Data

MacGregor, Geddes.
The Nicene creed, illumined by modern thought.
1.   Nicene Creed.   I.   Title.
BT999.M32   238'.142   80-19348
ISBN 0-8028-1855-2

Contents

Preface

THE Nicene Creed was finally accepted at the Council of Constantinople in the year 381. I conceived the present little book and had it under contract with my publishers before noticing how apposite would be the date of publication: the eve of 1981, when thoughtful Christians all over the world would be celebrating the sixteen-hundredth anniversary of that historic event in the history of the Christian Church. I am happy to make a small contribution to the thought of all who prize that formulation of the apostolic faith and wish to reaffirm their own faith in its terms with even better understanding than before. The Nicene Fathers, like the cathedral builders of a much later age, built better than they could have known, for Nicene orthodoxy, interpreted in the light of the liveliest contemporary thought, stands today as a bulwark against those who would water down Christianity into a social ethic that is not even good civil religion and certainly not as much as a ghost of authentic Christian faith. May God write the Nicene Creed into the hearts of Christians today and illumine their minds with a vision of what it means for personal salvation and the destiny of humankind.

As scholars know well, the text of the Creed, no less than that of the New Testament, has varied in some details in medieval manuscripts as well as in usage elsewhere. The Greek and English texts I cite are, however, standard ones.

—GEDDES MACGREGOR

The Greek Text

Πιστεύω εἰς ἕνα Θεὸν Πατέρα παντοκράτορα ποιητὴν οὐρανοῦ καὶ γῆς ὁρατῶν τε πάντων καὶ ἀοράτων. καὶ εἰς ἕνα κύριον Ἰησοῦν Χριστόν τὸν υἱὸν τοῦ Θεοῦ τὸν μονογενῆ τὸν ἐκ τοῦ Πατρὸς γεννηθέντα πρὸ πάντων τῶν αἰώνων, φῶς ἐκ φωτός, θεὸν ἀληθινὸν ἐκ θεοῦ ἀληθινοῦ, γεννηθέντα οὐ ποιηθέντα, ὁμοούσιον τῷ Πατρί· δι' οὗ τὰ πάντα ἐγένετο· τὸν δι' ἡμᾶς τοὺς ἀνθρώπους καὶ διὰ τὴν ἡμετέραν σωτηρίαν κατελθόντα ἐκ τῶν οὐρανῶν καὶ σαρκωθέντα ἐκ Πνεύματος ἁγίου καὶ Μαρίας τῆς παρθένου καὶ ἐνανθρωπήσαντα, σταυρωθέντα τε ὑπὲρ ἡμῶν ἐπὶ Ποντίου Πιλάτου καὶ παθόντα καὶ ταφέντα καὶ ἀναστάντα τῇ τρίτῃ ἡμέρᾳ κατὰ τὰς γραφὰς καὶ ἀνελθόντα εἰς τοὺς οὐρανοὺς καὶ καθεζόμενον ἐκ δεξιῶν τοῦ Πατρὸς καὶ πάλιν ἐρχόμενον μετὰ δόξης κρῖναι ζῶντας καὶ νεκρούς· οὗ τῆς βασιλείας οὐκ ἔσται τέλος. καὶ εἰς τὸ Πνεῦμα τὸ ἅγιον τὸ κύριον τὸ ζωοποιὸν τὸ ἐκ τοῦ Πατρὸς ἐκπορευόμενον τὸ σὺν Πατρὶ καὶ Υἱῷ συμπροσκυνούμενον καὶ συνδοξαζόμενον τὸ λαλῆσαν διὰ τῶν προφητῶν. εἰς μίαν ἁγίαν καθολικὴν καὶ ἀποστολικὴν ἐκκλησίαν· ὁμολογῶ ἓν βάπτισμα εἰς ἄφεσιν ἁμαρτιῶν· προσδοκῶ ἀνάστασιν νεκρῶν καὶ ζωὴν τοῦ μέλλοντος αἰῶνος. ἀμήν.

Traditional English Translation

I believe in one God the Father Almighty, Maker of heaven and earth, And of all things visible and invisible:

And in one Lord Jesus Christ, the only-begotten Son of God, Begotten of his Father before all worlds, God of God, Light of Light, Very God of very God, Begotten, not made, Being of one substance with the Father, By whom all things were made: Who for us men and for our salvation came down from heaven, And was incarnate by the Holy Ghost of the Virgin Mary, And was made man, And was crucified also for us under Pontius Pilate. He suffered and was buried, And the third day he rose again according to the Scriptures, And ascended into heaven, And sitteth on the right hand of the Father. And he shall come again with glory to judge both the quick and the dead: Whose kingdom shall have no end.

And I believe in the Holy Ghost, The Lord and giver of life, Who proceedeth from the Father [and the Son], Who with the Father and the Son together is worshipped and glorified, Who spake by the Prophets. And I believe one Catholick and Apostolick Church. I acknowledge one Baptism for the remission of sins. And I look for the Resurrection of the dead, And the Life of the world to come. Amen.

Introduction

THE Nicene Creed is the symbol *par excellence* of Christian orthodoxy. Its language is antique, befitting the mold of its thought. Yet, if a formulation of classic Church teaching is to be found anywhere, it is to be found here. It provides the best focus for our study of traditional orthodoxy illumined by modern scientific knowledge. After the inevitable controversies that had attended early discussion of how the Bible should be interpreted, the Nicene Creed emerged as a convenient summary of what the Church took to be the best way of expressing the essence of the gospel that the apostles had proclaimed.

To suggest that the Nicene Creed came out of the deliberations of that great assembly held in the year 325, the Council of Nicaea, would be natural but misleading. The creed we call Nicene has a history too long and too complex to be recounted here; nor would such an account serve our purpose. A brief note will suffice. This creed in its present form was probably accepted by the Council of Constantinople in 381. Thus, scholars sometimes call it the Nicene-Constantinopolitan Creed. After its complex history, it was recognized by the great Council of Chalcedon in 451 and has been taken ever since to be the embodiment of Christian orthodoxy.

We are to look at the Nicene Creed in the light of our contemporary scientific thinking. Nevertheless, in order to do that usefully, we must take care never to lose sight of the historical circumstances in which it was put together and issued. To say that it addressed itself to its time seems a truism, since everything intelligible that anyone ever says must be said within the intellectual climate of the age in which it is spoken. Yet many overlook the implications of that obvious fact. On the one hand, those who see little value in classic orthodoxy are disposed to dismiss the Creed as a mere antiquarian curiosity. On the other hand, those who do attach great importance to fidelity to the ancient heritage of the Church sometimes feel they must utter it uncritically, singing it with tuneful zest since they cannot profess it in any way with understanding.

If, however, it does contain eternal truth and if it does indeed enshrine the essence of the apostolic faith in the antique reliquary of its language, surely the Creed may be more amenable to being reconciled to contemporary scientific truths than are the creeds of those who seek to bring God into line with contemporary fashion by cutting eternal truth down to the size of the vanishing moment. Nothing is more irrelevant, when we are looking for eternal truth, than the sort of box that truth comes in: quaintly archaic or stridently up-to-date. If we were seriously looking for intellectual vigor, moral integrity, and spiritual vivacity, we would surely applaud their presence in a blind old cripple and deplore their absence in an athletic young man.

Two very different errors contribute to much modern misunderstanding of the Nicene Creed. One is the use, sometimes unconscious, of outmoded (even pre-Newtonian) scientific models to criticize what the Creed says. The other is the tendency to read the ancient formulation in terms of commonplace ways of thinking that have become habitual and that at best impoverish and at worst misrepresent its meaning. Our task must be therefore to show how surprisingly ready for marriage are this ancient symbol of Christian orthodoxy and the new ways of scientific thinking that have emerged from the twentieth-century revolution in scientific thought. Nothing anyone could say would ever prove the affirmations of the Nicene Creed as one proves Pythagoras's theorem. However, Christian orthodoxy can be defended better with tools forged from modern science than with any other ones that have been available since the Nicene Creed was formulated sixteen hundred years ago. Also, the Nicene Creed is much less wedded to the fashions of its day than is commonly supposed. Its affirmations do not depend fundamentally on the scientific ideas of the fourth or fifth or nineteenth centuries. In fact, an openminded application of our contemporary scientific thought might well foster appreciation of the Nicene Creed more than would an application of the scientific thought of our forefathers. That is part of what I hope to show.

My aim, however, goes beyond that. If the faith of Nicaea needed bolstering by appeal to contemporary scientific methods or discoveries, then the Creed would not be what it purports to be: a summary and enunciation of the fundamental truths God has revealed for appropriation by men and women of every generation, irrespective not only of race and color, poverty and wealth, but also of time in the sequence of human history, truths to be appropriated everywhere, in all ages, and by all. So the faith of Nicaea is a catalyst for contemporary thought, challenging some of our outmoded presuppositions while provoking us to richer understanding of what Christians for so many centuries have so lovingly and joyfully proclaimed as the mainspring of their lives.

CHAPTER I

Faith

I believe in

IF we were to ask the average person why the Creed begins with the words "I believe" rather than "I know," he or she would probably answer that religious people are not expected to *know*. In contrast to scientists, who have to know, religious people must be content to *believe*. Such a person, seeing belief as a weak substitute for knowledge, would go on to account religious people's claim to mere belief a suitably and commendably modest one. Such a person would probably see the history of science as a steady progress in the accumulation of human knowledge, proceeding with the logic of a basic geometry text.

Such people, however, would be radically wrong both in their assumption of the religious person's modesty and in the confidence (not to say arrogance) they attribute to the creative scientist. The claim implied in the opening words of the Nicene Creed is, we shall see, a claim to a *kind* of knowledge, while no scientist worth his or her salt claims any sort of finality to such advancement in human knowledge as may have been made at this or that stage in the development of his or her scientific field. Scientific knowledge does not advance at all steadily. For every hypothesis that is verified by experiment, thousands are not. Furthermore, scientific theories that seemed beyond question two hundred years ago or less have since been supplanted by others that better fit our general understanding of the universe.

A comparison of the history of science with the history of Christian thought shows the forces of conservatism equally at

1

work. Lord Russell, in his *Religion and Science,* found plenty of scope for poking fun at religious ideophobia. He cites, for instance, the Greek Orthodox rule that sponsors at baptism, who might very well happen to fall in love and wish to marry, are precluded from doing so on the ground that they have acquired a spiritual affinity. That rule may seem typically obscurantist, but scientists have made similarly foolish conclusions. Aristotle, for long preeminent for his work in the sciences, thought a child's being born female was the result of a prevailing south wind at the time of conception. Much nearer our own time, Louis Pasteur, when trying to establish a connection between bacteria and disease, met opposition primarily from his scientific colleagues rather than from devout churchgoers. Scientists who know anything of the history of their field are well aware of the limitations of scientific knowledge.

Religious people as such do in fact make a more profound sort of claim to knowledge, though the more perceptive among them see that their grasp of the significance of their claim is enhanced with their experience of life. From books and friends a girl may learn something of what motherhood actually entails, and she believes what she learns. When a mother, she finds her belief transformed by an awareness of its personal significance, but the belief is not fundamentally changed. She knew from childhood, though she might have said, thoughtfully and modestly, only that she believed. The distinction between belief and knowledge need not be either as sharp as it seems in popular parlance or as subtle as some analytical philosophers nowadays try to make it.

Analytical philosophers have also made a distinction between "believing in" and "believing that." We must look at this distinction, since the Creed opens with the words "I believe *in.*" When I say that I believe *that* it is going to rain, I certainly do not mean that I believe in rain as I believe in peace or fair trade. Likewise, when I say that I believe *in* swimming, I am not simply asserting that swimming occurs; I am saying that it is good for me to swim, and I might possibly be suggesting that it could also be good for you. So, when I say that I believe in my student Bob Smith, I do not mean that I recognize and take account of his existence. I am saying, rather, that I think he shows promise and will eventually make his mark, or something of that sort.

Nevertheless, the distinction is not as clear as at first sight it looks. If we were to insist on it, then when you asked me whether I believed in dragons and I replied no, I would have had to mean this: "While I know that dragons may exist, I have no trust in them." That would have been in fact, of course, not at all what I had meant. I would have meant simply that I do not believe that dragons exist.

We shall see over and over again that the Nicene Creed does not make distinctions such as these, which have been invented in modern philosophical discussion for specific and sometimes narrow and trivial purposes. The Greek words *pistis* (faith) and *pisteuein* (to believe) have the same root. The New Testament usage here follows an Old Testament mode of thought in which Abraham's belief in God is simply his sure trust in God's promise.

Our difficulty here, as it is so often elsewhere in our attempts to understand the Nicene Creed and other such documents, lies in getting behind the complexities of our modern thought to the comparative simplicity of that of the past. Complex in some respects, past thought is in others too simple for us to grasp. Acceptance of the restrictive distinctions of specialized types of modern thought obscures the meaning of the Creed as adherence to traditionalist science has often hindered scientific advance.

The Nicene Creed expresses an act of faith. That faith implies "belief that" but entails much more. When you promise me something and I say, "I believe you," I mean, "I believe that you will keep your promise, for I believe in your moral integrity." Suppose you promised to pay back a loan you proposed. You might have persuaded me to rely on your word by providing collateral for that loan, enabling me to seize your property if you broke your promise. Then I should have no need to consider whether I could trust you or not. But, when I say I believe you, I am not merely saying that I am satisfied with the business arrangements proposed; I am saying that you have somehow or other succeeded in convincing me of your moral integrity. I do not merely believe that you will repay me, collateral or no; I believe you are the sort of person I can trust, the sort of person who will never let me down.

That is what, in an absolute sense, the opening words of the Nicene Creed say about our belief in God. Because of what God has unfolded about himself in the course of our life experience, short or long, we who subscribe to the Creed are convinced that our reliance on God is in every way justified. Our reliance is not a blind act of the will as in the old schoolboy definition of faith ("believing steadfastly what you know ain't true"); it is a recognition that God is absolutely trustworthy. Plainly, this implies that he exists. It would be silly to say I put infinite trust in him and then to add that I believe he exists. It would be somewhat like my telling you that I have loved my wife for twenty years and then adding that I believe she exists. That is one reason why many theologians today say that existence is too weak a category to be applied to God.

Faith in God is an affirmation of one's whole being. In making the affirmation I testify that my total life experience leads me to the conclusion that God is at the "deep core" of all things *and that the situation could not be otherwise.* It is not as though I were saying that I happen to have had a kind father and am glad to be able so to report, since I know of many people whose fathers have been despicable rotters.

The word *God,* however, is notoriously ambiguous. Were it not, then the Creed might well stop with that word instead of going on as it does with a list of qualifiers. It goes on with these qualifiers because otherwise *God* could be taken to mean almost anything. It might refer, for instance, to the god preeminent in the Greek or Egyptian pantheon. It might mean simply "the way things are." It might mean the sum of all things, including my typewriter, the planet Uranus, my dream last night, and the Vice-President of the United States. It might very well mean my own aspirations or ideals. It might even mean yours, for maybe I admired yours and wished to make them my own. On the contrary, however, it means something sufficiently specific to need all the qualifiers and entailments and specifications set out in the Creed.

The assertion of belief in God is, then, both moral and intellectual. Broadly speaking, if we were to distinguish Catholic tradition from that of the heirs of the Reformation, we might say that the former has tended to stress the intellectual aspect and the latter the volitional aspect, including the moral implications of fidelity and trust, though many exceptions could be found. At any rate, the two aspects are in fact two sides of the same coin. They are both aspects of what faith entails. However, some interpretations of the Creed are indeed inadequate or misguided or worse, simply because they diminish or water down one or the other or both of these aspects. For example, some people talk of formulations such as the Nicene Creed as though they were pleasantly antique expressions of our feelings toward the human situation, encumbered though they be with not only quaint verbiage but also outmoded concepts and attitudes. To say that sort of thing, whether with a superior air or otherwise, is to misunderstand any useful function of the Nicene Creed, besides of course traducing the intention of those who formulated it. The psychologism in such attitudes leads to the worst kind of misunderstanding. It is as though someone were to say: "I like the way scientists talk about planetary orbits. It appeals to my aesthetic sense. Besides, it gives people on Earth a less parochial outlook than we might otherwise have. Also, thinking in that way puts my psyche in good shape. So I approve of it in every way, and I hope schools will go on teaching it, though of course I don't believe for a moment that planets do actually behave that way."

We have seen that the Nicene Creed expresses an act of faith, and we have also seen that faith is often contrasted with knowledge. While faith is certainly not knowledge like the knowledge I have of my cousin's telephone number or of the number of buttons on my jacket or even of the presence of my daughter in the room, it is knowledge *of a kind:* an inductive kind. A parallel, though not an exact one, is the knowledge that a creative scientist has when he believes he is on to something. He postulates something (say, radium), makes a hypothesis, and then seeks to verify it to the satisfaction of his colleagues in the scientific societies. Pasteur, for instance, in some sense knew that his theory about the relation between bacteria and disease was correct, though he had not yet proved it to his colleagues' satisfaction. It must have distressed him to see a surgeon pick up an instrument from the floor where he had dropped it and proceed to operate.

So, when Abraham went out "not knowing whither he went," he was not so entirely ignorant of where he was going as are we all of, say, the chemistry of planets in the outer galaxies. He was not so ignorant as am I of the topography of Tierra del Fuego. Yet the knowledge with which he did set out on his journey was so meager that his act took moral courage. So it is that we are called upon to go through life. We are by no means walking in total darkness; indeed, we know a great deal about our environment and about how to cope with life's contingencies; nevertheless, we certainly do not see our way all the time with perfect clarity. Accidents happen; tragedies occur; my most cherished and carefully laid plans go wrong; yet, despite all that, I generally proceed in a fairly confident frame of mind. What I know of life, all its miseries and disappointments notwithstanding, buoys me up with the will to go on, reinforcing my belief that my way of looking at things is right in principle and, on the whole, warrants my confidence.

An obvious objection arises here. Till as recently as 1628, when Harvey's treatise changed older medical presuppositions about the heart and the arteries, physicians had acted for centuries on the assumption that blood does not circulate throughout the body. Generation after generation they had been wrong, and their treatments must have been vitiated by that ignorance. May not Christians have been similarly wrong in their adherence to the Nicene Creed? To answer this question we must first notice that medical people were not *totally* wrong about the nature and structure of the body. While ignorant of much, they were also knowledgeable of much. Through the medical experience and scientific inquiry of the past, they had acquired a certain corpus of medical learning and skill, but they had to keep open to new discoveries that would further enlighten them. Christians, who believe they are the recipients of an unfolding of God in the Bible and that the Nicene Creed provides a summary of how the Church has most profitably interpreted that biblical revelation, must not fall into the error of worshipping the words of the Creed, an act that would be idolatrous; they ought to see in those words a mine whence they may dig ever-new kinds of precious ore. They should welcome every fresh human discovery, not least in sciences such as biology and physics, for the enlightenment it may bring and especially for the fuller appropriation of the significance of the Creed that it may make possible.

A well-known example of the illumination that science has brought to religion is the effect of the evolutionary theories of Darwin and Huxley in the second half of the nineteenth century on those Christian thinkers who chose to be enlightened by them. In effect, what those Christian thinkers said was this: "We accepted the traditional view that God had created species of life (birds, fish, mammals) distinctly and separately, and that he did so in distinct and separate periods of time, called in the Bible 'days.' We praised him for so creating the universe as described in Genesis 1. Now we listen to the scientists of our day and are persuaded that the evolutionary principle operates all through nature. This discovery immensely enhances our appreciation of God's creative act. It is far more wonderful than we had thought." Genesis is not wrong; it sets forth the account of creation in a simplistic, childish way. Now thoughtful people who read it can see how it points to a far grander state of affairs than had hitherto been known.

Other Christian thinkers who said, rather, that the Genesis story must be read literally, so that either you believed or disbelieved it "as is," are like people who, on discovering that Dante had not actually been on a subterranean journey, had never emerged at the antipodes of Jerusalem, and had never ascended the seven-storeyed mountain, either cry out in disappointment that Dante was a liar and not to be trusted or else insist that, whatever geophysicists and others might say about his alleged travels, they would go on believing that hell is as conical in shape as Dante said it was and that, if only we knew more precisely the dimensions of the earth, we could conduct a survey enabling us to discover the entrance and confirm that the fearful words inscribed upon it are written in Italian as he claimed. Indeed, Dante himself would have been ill disposed to find himself taken so literally. The learned of the Middle Ages were accustomed to allegorize and to be allegorically understood. They knew too much about the many dimensions of reality to suppose it could be squeezed into a single level of language. This did not mean that men and women of faith in those days believed less ardently or sincerely. On the contrary, they were capable of the most passionate and vigorous belief. By seeing beyond the words of the Creed, we do not necessarily water it down. We may indeed be enriching it, and that is what I hope to do. If we approach our task with loving hearts and open minds, we shall find far more in the Creed when we have finished than do those who thoughtlessly accept it.

Authentic faith is grounded in belief. We cannot trust God till we believe in him. Yet faith is much more than belief. The man

or woman who is able to walk through life with that strong trust in
God that comes from active faith can do so only because of a heart
that is open, loving, and free. If I had perfect faith, I should be
completely fearless (cf. I John 4:18). Even a little faith can do
wonders (Matthew 17:20; Luke 17:6). The Christian pilgrim, the
"knight of faith," becomes increasingly aware of God's care and
guidance as he or she recognizes the guiding hand of God in the
past, in situations in which he or she had been largely unaware of
such guidance. Trust in God does not mean the slightest diminu-
tion of human effort; on the contrary, it intensifies that effort.
Nothing, however, is more necessary for a happy life than an
increase of faith. Like muscle, it develops with exercise. When we
say the opening words of the Creed, we should say them not only
with our minds, not only with our hearts, but with every fibre of
our being : "I believe!"

*ALMIGHTY and everlasting God, who hast revealed thy
glory by Christ, among all nations, preserve the works of thy
mercy; that thy Church, which is spread throughout the
world, may persevere with steadfast faith in confession of thy
Name; through Jesus Christ our Lord.—Amen.*

—Gelasian Sacramentary,
Office for Good Friday (fifth century)

---CHAPTER II---

Ground of All Process

One God the Father Almighty

IN the Nicene Creed the word *one* before the word *God* is emphatic. Historically, the intention was not to affirm that God exists, for in the ancient world that would have been generally accounted a platitude, somewhat like our saying that energy exists. Of course energy exists; of course, as an early Greek sage had said, "the world is full of gods." In the ancient world, any wonder, any remarkable power, could be called a *theos*, a god. Some of these powers or gods were more enduring than others; some were comparatively trivial and local, such as an unusually gusty wind around one of the islands of Greece, while others were far more overwhelming and fearsome, besides being always there in greater or lesser degree.

Everyone knows, for instance, how tremendously powerful in human affairs is our sexuality; so Venus, Roman goddess of love, who personified sex, was a very great deity indeed. To a young man or woman in love she would seem the greatest. When, in a festal procession, her image or statue appeared on the scene, the lovers would hail her more enthusiastically than they would any other. But then one is not in love all the time. Sometimes, for instance, when national honor is affronted and the people are sufficiently infuriated, Mars, the god of war, gains the limelight. During a long period of peace he may seem to many to have declined very much in power, but now, like a modern film star who has seemed to retire and then suddenly stages a dramatic comeback, Mars returns with all the fury and cruelty and promises of glory that attend his presence.

The question, then as now, is not Do you believe in God? but, rather, What kind of God do you believe in? The Nicene Creed specifically and pointedly affirms belief in one Being at the core of all things, a Being who is not merely supreme, presiding over all other powers, but who is both the source of all other powers and the magnet that draws all other beings into orbit, as planets orbit their sun.

The meaning of this affirmation cannot be properly understood apart from its alternative, which, for the ancients, was a pluralism of powers. The pantheon, or governing board of gods as we might call it, was an aristocracy of powers, all vying for mastery, all endlessly politicking in one way or another, all having ups and downs, none definitively succeeding. One of them might gain an impressive ascendancy over the others, as did Zeus among the Greek gods, for instance; but as grand and exalted as was his position, he was still no more than a strong and mighty president over the pantheon, having to deal with the intrigues of the other deities and being from time to time involved in their love affairs. Even a Zeus could be dethroned, at least in theory, for his power was supreme only in the sense in which that of a czar or modern dictator is supreme. In such a system, no one's power could be, strictly speaking, absolute.

We may smile at the absurdities of such primitive beliefs. So did the Greek philosophers and the wise men in Israel centuries before the birth of Christ. Today we tend to think that civilized people have gone far beyond such ways of looking at the universe and the human situation, that the question for us could never be the same one to which the authors of the Nicene Creed were addressing themselves. For us, we suppose, the question must be on a different (not to say higher) plane: "Assuming the monotheistic understanding of God as presented in the Jewish, Christian, and Muslim traditions, do we believe in such a Being or do we not?" In fact, however, the question relevant to our contemporary ways of thought is not at all so different from the one to which the Nicene Fathers addressed themselves. Few people today, Jews, Christians, or Muslims, who do not take their respective traditions seriously, could be called "atheists" as that term is understood today in its technical, modern sense.

Such people are not saying there is nothing to be worshipped; on the contrary, they are saying that indeed all sorts of powers around us (money and poverty, health and disease, knowledge and ignorance, love and hate, and perhaps even the signs of the zodiac and other astrological circumstances) govern our lives. Far from ignoring those powers, we had better use all the political acumen we can muster to learn how to cope with them so as to make them work for rather than against us. And that, of course, is precisely what the Nicene Fathers were opposing by their affirmation: "one God, the Father Almighty." All other powers, be they conceived as angels or saints or the powers of nature, can never be more than the agencies of this one God, the Father Almighty.

The use of the metaphorical term *Father* is less important than the use of the word *one*. *One* is what is proclaimed in the home of every observant Jew and in every synagogue today: "Hear, O Israel, the Lord thy God is One." It is the central affirmation proclaimed by the muezzin from the minaret of every mosque. It is also the ground of every specifically Christian belief, the focus apart from which nothing else in Christian faith makes any sense at all. The use of the term *Father*, by contrast, was primarily conventional. Zeus was habitually called "Father Zeus"; his name, indeed, is the Greek counterpart of the Indian Dyaush Pitar, "the Sky Father." Plato calls God "Father and Maker of the universe." The Bible calls God "Father." It is a natural epithet, not only in every society, patriarchal or otherwise, that is structured upon the family, but in any society at all, since every child needs and longs for a father, whether he or she has an available living male parent or not.

The use of this metaphor does not become habitual in the Bible till comparatively late. It occurs, for instance, in the Psalms, but it is not characteristic. In the later books of the Old Testament, however, it becomes not only a characteristic term for God, but one invested with the deep emotional significance of one who protects and loves his children, for whom he has the fullest personal, moral responsibility. This usage, adopted as a matter of course in the New Testament, is also developed as the one appropriate to the relationship of God as the ground of Being to Jesus Christ, who is acclaimed as the unique Son of the Father. So a typical New Testament phrase is "God the Father of our Lord Jesus Christ." Christians are encouraged to say "Abba" (the child's first loving recognition of his father, expressed in baby talk) in address-ing God, for Jesus Christ himself so prayed and he has made us adopted sons of his Father. The term *Father* expresses in the simplest of language the relationship of love revealed to us through Christ. What still remains emphatic, however, is that we are talking of the *one* God, the *one* Father: him who is the source of all things.

We now come to the other attribute of God expressed in the Nicene Creed: the almightiness. Not only is God the one source of all things and the magnet that draws all beings towards him, but he is also the supreme controller of all events. The term used in the Creed is *pantokratōr*, which means "ruler of all things." This term, familiar to the Greek Church to this day as the basic designa-tion of God, has the connotation of being at the helm, as is a good skipper. When the Bible and the Creed were translated into Latin, the term chosen as equivalent was *omnipotens*, from which we derive the English word *omnipotent*, which carries with it the magical notion of "able to do anything" or "you name it: he can do it." This is not at all what the original Greek says. The notion that God can do anything (such as stopping a bullet in the middle of its trajectory, or enabling you to pass an examination in which you have just received an announcement of your failure, or mak-ing Aunt Bessie's death not to have happened when it has hap-pened) is both ridiculous and less than we ought to expect of God, to whom we should ascribe the power to help us solve our prob-lems in ways far more wonderful than those suggested in child-ishly fanciful notions such as these.

Moreover, the Latin poets ascribed omnipotence in a loose sense to various deities as a general term of glorification. And similar terms of glorification have been applied to various earthly potentates: James the First of Great Britain, for example, for whom the King James Version of the English Bible is named, was addressed as "Most High and Mighty Prince" and "Most Dread Sovereign." Adulatory terms, such as "Brightest Star of the Fir-mament" and "Most Exalted Monarch," have been customary forms of polite address to those earthly rulers who have not always seen fit to discourage sycophancy among their subjects. The use of the term *omnipotent* is, for these and other reasons, singularly unfortunate, not least because it says only something unspecific

and childishly flattering when it should be saying something notably specific, namely, that the one God who is acclaimed is absolutely
in charge of all things and in control of all possible events. God
controls the history in which he acts. He has a definite purpose.
This does not mean that we are left without any freedom of
choice. On the contrary, the most crucial choices in our personal
lives are in our hands, as well as are the trivial ones. Not only
are we free to decide what color drapes to hang in the living room,
we are also free to live selflessly or selfishly, free to say yes or no
to Christ, free to love justice or to hate it. Our personal freedom is
not, however, unlimited. That would be absurd. Unlimited freedom would mean that I am free to jump over the moon, when in
fact I can jump only a few feet at best. Even nihilistic existen-
tialists, such as Jean-Paul Sartre, who stress human freedom, recognize that freedom is circumscribed by circumstances. I am free,
yet I cannot change the date or place of my birth or choose parents
other than my own. I get certain circumstances, certain tools, and I
am free to do what I can with them.

The power of God, as understood by the authors of the
Creed, is the power of love. God does not force us to choose one
course of action over another; he lets us be, leaving us free to make
or mar our destinies by our choices. His rule of the world is the
rule of love. In the exercise of rule by love there are no easy
shortcuts. A Hitler, a Henry VIII, or any political dictator can chop
off a few heads to gain a supposed temporary convenience or ad-
vantage, but in the rule of love the ointment for the healing of
humankind is far more expensive and far more permanently effec-
tive. That is the truth enshrined in the line of Friedrich von Logau
translated by Longfellow and rooted in an ancient Greek proverb:
"though the mills of God grind slowly, yet they grind exceeding
small." Both God's justice and his love take a long time to work
out; but in the end his rule of love, which is inseparable from his
purpose, is always successful. God, who is "the Lord of hosts,"
that is, the Lord over all powers, good or evil, in the universe,
conquers all through the rule of love, the costliest of all forms of
government.

Such is basic Christian belief. Is there anything in contemporary scientific knowledge to justify it? Certainly nothing in physics
or chemistry could ever conceivably provide specific support for

any such world view. Love such as is envisioned in the Bible and the Creed does not come within the domain of these sciences. Scientists can tell us nothing that could either support or collapse this basic Christian belief. Biology, which does show the advantages for survival in renouncing mere tooth-and-claw modes of living in favor of ones that entail the discipline and give-and-take of organization and community, does point in the direction of a Christian understanding, but only in the vaguest and most rudimentary way. The notion that might is right seems only too often justified by the facts, not least at the lower levels of biological development, in which the strong seem to exercise absolute power over the weak.

In the human condition, which represents the highest we know from empirical observation on our planet, we have learned to put the brakes on naked power; yet the brakes too often give out, and the consequences of even the most minor and temporary failure of these moral brakes can be catastrophic for humankind. Moreover, humankind itself, as we know so well nowadays, lives a highly precarious existence. Not only could it exhaust the energy needed for its biological survival; it could also very easily, in some circumstances, annihilate itself by the terrible nuclear weapons of its own design. Never with more reason has humanity's pessimism about its future seemed more warranted.

From the social sciences we do get some more pointed hints of the power of love within human relationships. Through the study of psychology we learn, for instance, something of the unparalleled power of love in circumstances that otherwise seem virtually hopeless. The sick child whose case seems medically grave and probably terminal can sometimes be astonishingly restored to health by the power of an overwhelming love. Under the influence of a deeply genuine love, human quarrels can be mended and disasters averted. All that is true, and no one with any experience of life would deny it. Yet tragedy does strike at humanity, whatever dispositions seem to be prevailing. It strikes with a seeming cruelty and arbitrariness that shock our consciences. The fact that it shocks us tells us much about ourselves and the nobility of our ideals and expectations but nothing about the state of affairs in the universe and certainly nothing about the nature of God.

In parapsychology we find much clearer pointers to the reality of divine love and the benevolence of divine purpose. Comparatively few Christians, however, feel the need or even the desire to probe deeply into such fields of inquiry for enlightenment, and since even the most zealous exponents of parapsychological inquiry would readily admit the limitations of the knowledge they claim, most Christians must fall back on the conviction that comes to us through the response of faith to the revelation of the Bible and on the attestation of faith among those who throughout the ages have known even more trouble and affliction than have we ourselves, for assurance that at the core of the universe is One who is at the helm, *pantokratōr*, ruling effectively through his reign of love, which always in the end prevails. Such a belief entails certain corollaries, which remain to be discussed in later chapters. All these corollaries, however, depend on this basic view of what lies at the core of all things.

Yet when all that is said, an all-important fact remains to be stated. Although the sciences cannot in themselves provide support for the Christian view, modern scientific thought does make such a view more plausible than it was in a mechanistic age, in which the model of a machine was adopted for the universe and hence for the human being who is a microcosmic universe of his or her own. More will be said about this in the next chapter, in which we will consider the relationship between what we call nature and what we call God. There we shall also begin to see in what way contemporary scientific thought is much more hospitable to the beliefs proclaimed in orthodox Christianity than is generally understood by those who are too overawed by the technological applications of the sciences to appreciate either the nature of Christian thought or the limitations of scientific discovery.

WE praise thee, O God:
We acknowledge thee to be the Lord.
All the earth doth worship thee: the Father everlasting.
                    —Ascribed to Niceta of Remesiana
                              (fifth century)

CHAPTER III

Nature and God

Maker of heaven and earth,
and of all things visible and invisible

IN the minds of those modern thinkers, scientists or philosophers, who take Christian orthodoxy seriously, the assertion that God is the "maker" of the universe raises a fundamental question, perhaps indeed *the* fundamental question for the reconciliation of the sciences and religion.

In the history of Western thought the term *nature* has had a wide variety of meanings. As used by modern scientists, it usually signifies the general order to be found in the universe, the aggregate of entities that are or can be observed, including humanity. The modern scientist recognizes order, regularity, and predictability in the universe; but he or she is also confronted with a no less noteworthy randomness, not least in quantum theory and in biology, of which mutation of the genes and the operation of natural selection are examples. Scientific "laws," so called, are descriptions of the invariancies the scientist abstracts from his or her observation of nature.

When we say God "made" all things, we must ask in what sense we are to understand this "making." The traditional way of stating the "making" was to say that God created everything "out of nothing." For certain historical reasons, Christian thinkers felt it peculiarly important to avoid saying anything suggestive of the notion that the universe flows from or emanates from God, as a river flows from the spring. That notion was felt to be a betrayal of

the intention of the biblical writers, who think with the characteristically Semitic emphasis on will and decision and lack the
Greek preoccupation with the quest for knowledge. God had to be
represented as clearly making a free decision to do something he
need not have done and that his having left undone would not have
diminished in any way his self-contained happiness.
That theological concern with bringing out the notion of
creative decision and with distinguishing it from pouring forth or
emanating was commendable. Yet it did make the notion of the
divine act and the relation between God and the universe peculiarly difficult for thinking people. Many of the prominent thinkers of the early part of the present century who were not in principle averse to the concept of God (including, for instance, Einstein)
found that way of seeing the relation between God and the universe unacceptable if not unintelligible. Some, such as Whitehead,
would have preferred to look on the relation between God and the
Universe as did Plato in the *Timaeus:* God works on some sort of
primordial stuff. Many theologians, however, resisted interpretations of that sort, not only because they seemed unbiblical but also
because they seemed to make God only one of two eternal entities.
No doubt long before then intelligent people must have been
perplexed by the notion that God made something, let alone everything, out of nothing. The reflective housewife, as she sat in
her pew in church, might have said to herself, "I make pancakes
because my husband and family need to be fed and we all like
pancakes, so I buy the ingredients and make them. God apparently
makes things out of nothing; but why does he make anything at all
when he doesn't have to? The preacher says it's because he loves
us; but he got along without us in the first place when we weren't
there, so how can he be said to love what he neither had nor
needed?"
        A more sophisticated person before the present century,
perhaps an engineer or physics teacher, who knew something of
the nature of the universe as Newton and others had presented it,
would have put the question a little differently. Such a person, in
the same church pew, might have been thinking: "The universe is
a very fine machine, like a clock, but far more complicated. It had
to be constructed somehow. God apparently was the engineer, the
'grand architect,' who attended to the construction in the first

place and then set it going as I set going the grandfather clock in the hall with a flick of the pendulum. Of course, if I were making a clock like that, I should need wood and other materials. I couldn't make it out of thin air; but apparently God doesn't need even thin air. He just says, 'Let there be light,' and it appears, and 'Let there be kangaroos,' and they appear. This doesn't seem to fit what we know in physics. Still, the biologists of late have come up with the theory that we have evolved from lower forms of life, and that doesn't quite fit the laws of mechanics. The difference is that physicists and biologists seem to be able to talk to one another with some hope of mutual understanding, while what the Bible and the Church say do not fit anything we know. Still, church does seem to keep family and society together and, being a family man and a good citizen, I'm all for that, so I'll be in church next Sunday as usual.''

As things have turned out, however, what was chiefly wrong with the physics teacher's thinking was his physics. For whatever the universe is, it is now seen to be anything other than a machine. The whole scientific model of a vast machine with or without a divine engineer is as outmoded as the notion of God sitting up in heaven saying, "Let there be kangaroos." If any simple model could fit what physicists have learned about the universe today, it would have to be one in which the concepts of energy and mass played a leading role. It would use symbols of light and velocity rather than those of nuts and bolts. The universe, as Eddington suggested many decades ago, looks more like a thought than a machine. Yet to our forefathers of a century or two ago that would have seemed either an absurdity or a theological pipe dream.

Till the very end of the nineteenth century the old elec-tromagnetic theory of light had seemed virtually unassailable. Light had been seen to be unique; but in what did its uniqueness consist? Newton had thought that light was a rain of particles (what came to be called the corpuscular theory) emitted by the body emitting the light. Newton, extraordinarily careful observer and thinker though he was, rejected a notion put forward by Huygens to the effect that light moves in waves. He thought it must flow in straight lines, which is indeed what one would think from looking at the sharp boundaries of shadows. The tremendous advances that had occurred between Newton's time and the end of

the nineteenth century suggested, however, that on this point
Huygens had been right. Light does come in waves of various
lengths. So at one end of the spectrum we have infrared, with its
heating effects, and at the other end we have ultraviolet, beyond
which are the X-rays that Röntgen discovered in 1896, ushering in
the beginnings of radiation physics. Then in 1900 the most astonishing discovery so far came by Max Planck, revolutionizing
thought about the nature and structure of the universe and de-
manding, besides much else, a new understanding of the phrase
"all things visible and invisible."

Planck said it was necessary to assume that the emission and
absorption of light take place not in arbitrarily small amounts, as
the old theories had presupposed, but in *quanta*, which we might
call atoms. What made Planck's view so revolutionary was, from
one point of view, that it focused attention on the microcosmic, the
infinitesimal, rather than on the infinitely great. To see this possibility took very clear intellectual vision and creative insight. The
earliest scientists in the ancient world had been preoccupied with
infinity. The Greeks did not like the notion: they called it that
which has no bounds (*to apeiron*), and they tended to contrast
it unfavorably with that which has form (*morphos*). They thought
of the infinite as amorphous. After Planck's discovery, however,
scientists had to deal with a whole new world of atoms and mole-
cules, electrons and nuclei.

To primitive thought, all this comes as a shock, for most
primitive people and children think of God as big. I remember
that, as a very little boy, I imagined God to be at least two stories
high. In Mahayana Buddhism popular statuary often suggests
enormity. The Egyptians also often portrayed their gods in gigan-
tic form. A Frenchman is said to have suggested that an Englishman's God would be an Englishman twelve feet high. Such
conceptions of deity suggest visibility as a preeminent characteristic. What if God turned out to be infinitely small? In the seventeenth century, indeed, Blaise Pascal, one of the most deeply
Christian thinkers of all time, and one who happened to be also a
mathematician, had hinted that God might be conceived as a point
moving at infinite speed. Modern physics has shown that, if we are
to think of God at all, then perhaps Pascal's symbol is more apposite than the traditional ones.

Planck saw the minuteness of the discontinuity of the emission and absorption of light. Einstein, five years later, suggested, in effect, that Planck had not gone far enough. Light itself is discontinuous. It is "quantized." It *behaves* like a rain of particles as indeed Newton had proposed; yet they are not "real" particles in the sense of having mass. Since then physicists have investigated the connection between the number and velocity of the electrons emitted and the properties of light. By accurate measurements they have verified the correctness of what at first seemed startling new hypotheses.

What bearing does such a startling revolution in scientific thought have on the Nicene Creed? It certainly does not prove or disprove the existence of God. It does show, however, how traditional presuppositions about the universe can hamper and have hampered our thought about God. The obstacles had lain not primarily in anything that had been consciously inserted into thought about God but, rather, in something that had been taken for granted. For centuries people had assumed that the universe consists of a mass spread out in space and enduring in time. One then naturally went on to speculate: how much space? how much time? As one might ask how many tons of stone and how many years it took to build St. Paul's Cathedral, so if only one knew enough one could work out the weight of the universe and its construction time. What the scientific revolution showed above all was that these are the wrong questions, somewhat like asking how high is the sky.

Perhaps theologians and biblical scholars also needed to revolutionize their thinking. Such a revolution would have to do justice to whatever truths traditional theology had sought to preserve and that had found expression in the Nicene Creed and other formulations of Christian orthodoxy. For example, the resoluteness with which the classical theologians of the West, from Augustine to Thomas Aquinas and John Calvin, had insisted on creation contradistinguished from emanation might have been misplaced, being about a "right" answer to a wrong question.

The insistence by Karl Barth and other eminent Christian theologians that God is *totaliter aliter*, wholly other than the universe, reflects the biblical doctrine of the absolute dependence of the universe on God, its creator. People have generally read into this biblical doctrine the notion that God is an entity standing completely apart from the universe that he decided to make. In making it he made space and time. This way of thinking reflects an assumption that God must be *in all respects* different from his creation. Yet the river is absolutely dependent on the spring though by no means in all respects different from it. The difference between what we may call for our present purpose a Semitic way of thinking and a Greek one is not to be underestimated. If we put the question this way, Does God pour out the universe as the sun pours out sunshine or does he decide to bring it into being by an act of his will? then presumably any Christian who understands the problem and is committed to an orthodox view, rooted in the Bible, must choose unequivocally in favor of the latter alternative. But must we so put the question? Indeed, in the light of knowledge today, must we not, rather, avoid putting the question that way?

Of course I know and recognize the implications of the fact that, while I can be said to decide (if I believe in any sort of freedom of the will) whether or not to go to market, I cannot be said to decide whether or not to perspire on the way. I do that, as we say, naturally. The pores of my skin secrete sweat much as my liver secretes bile: it is an occurrence rather than my act. One might argue, indeed, whether such a distinction is clear, since I can hold back my tears and a good actor can make them flow at will. Be that as it may, can one usefully uphold such a distinction *on a cosmic scale?* Might not so putting the question about the divine act of creation be somewhat like talking of whether valleys are holes between mountains or mountains are walls on a valley's sides? Here as elsewhere in the Nicene Creed we should look more to what it denies than to what it seems to affirm. In that way we are less likely to be inserting our own presuppositions into it or to be coming down on this or that side of distinctions that are artifacts of our own making.

Christian thinkers from early times have emphasized the notion that God made the universe "out of nothing." This seems scientifically inconceivable and philosophically nonsensical. Thus both philosophers and scientists tend to say that, if we are to talk about God at all, we must think of his making the universe out of something, be it energy or air or play dough. "To make" *means* "to make out of something." But suppose we were to say that what the authors of the Creed intended was not to affirm that God made the universe out of nothing at all but to deny that he made it out of anything *other than himself?* One might object that if God made the universe out of himself he must have been thereby diminished. But am I diminished in giving you my love or even my thoughts? And do not I will so to do?

The notion that creation took place in the past and "at the beginning of time" is also one that calls for inspection. Even on a "big bang" theory of the origin of the universe, the view that the universe suddenly appeared, whether by divine fiat or otherwise, is surely by any reckoning a difficult one. It suggests the possibility that cosmic processes may be punctuated by big bangs for every new beginning but that we cannot be expected to take seriously the concept that, if only we knew enough, we could measure the age of the universe in so many "zillion" years and say that "before that there was nothing" or else that "before that there was nothing other than God." If such a notion were difficult in the past, it seems to have become impossible now, in the light of Einsteinian theories of the relativity of time and space.

People talked along such lines traditionally because the opening lines of Genesis seemed to justify no other way of understanding the situation. "In the beginning God created. . . . " In Greek and Latin, as in English, verbs specify tenses, actions that took place, are taking place, or will take place. Hebrew, however, has a different verb structure. The Hebrew verb indicates a state, not a tense. So the assertion in Hebrew is more ambiguous. More importantly still, while the English phrase "in the beginning" suggests a temporal event such as I would have in mind in saying that the clock struck ten as we entered the classroom and eleven as we left it, the biblical languages do not so imply a temporal connotation. The Greek *en archē* signifies something more like what I would intend by saying "archetypally." The phrase points beyond space and time. The notion that God is eternally engaged in creation is therefore more biblically orthodox than many have supposed it to be, and such a view is also one that accords better with what we have learned this century from scientific discovery.

Happily, the Nicene Creed makes no specification in favor of either a once-for-all or an eternally ongoing creation. At the outset, the Creed declares God to be *poiētēs ouranou:* he is the Maker. Later on it affirms a belief in Jesus Christ, being "of one substance" (*homoousios*) with the Father, *di' ou ta panta egeneto.* This last phrase, rendered in English "by whom all things were made," is what concerns us at the moment. It does not have the definite meaning the English suggests. It means only that all things (*ta panta*) have come into being by God. Its force is to reaffirm that, as the prologue to the Fourth Gospel says: "Nothing has been made without him," i.e., of course, without the Son.

So the Nicene Creed, provided that we do not read our own presuppositions and prejudices into it, is at this point eminently reconcilable with modern scientific discovery and thought. No less is it compatible with the view to which much contemporary theological reflection leads, that God, who is at the core of all things as their principle and source, enters into and travails with all things, visible and invisible.

The phrase "visible and invisible" or "seen and unseen" is particularly apposite to what contemporary physics has to tell us, for we now are dealing with a conception of the universe in which the most important subject matter of physics is indeed unseen. The Creed was composed at a time in which people were not so far removed as are we from the initial excitement of the discovery of what the mind, the "invisible" part of man, can do: the fact that through my imagination I can take off into a realm "within my-self" that seems not to depend on the senses. People of that age were still fascinated by the awareness that they could shut out their senses and enter into an interior world in which they could imagine people and horses and scenery that were not "there" in front of them, even what they had never seen and never expected to see or hear or touch or taste or smell. It was important for the authors of the Nicene Creed to include these interior phenomena along with the rest. They also intended to include, for example, the unseen powers: angels and other unseen ministers of God. They certainly knew nothing about either outer galaxies or the microcosmos of atoms and electrons of quantum physics. Yet, like the medieval cathedral builders who "built better than they knew," the authors of the Nicene Creed unwittingly made room in their formulation for what has become in our own century by far the most significant part of physics, to say nothing of the advances that have been made toward an understanding of the human psyche.

The purpose of the divine creativity goes therefore far beyond us human beings and our interests. This is a particularly important consideration, because it precludes all human-centered views of the purpose of the universe and all the old-fashioned notions that the universe exists for the benefit of this cosmic backwater we call the planet Earth. We humans are of course a part of the great evolutionary plan and purpose. We are "wonderfully made" indeed, as the Bible says. Yet we are by no means the end for which the process exists. We are not God's last word.

Other ancient religions have not always recognized this. Islam is taught in the Qur'ān to think otherwise. In that book, understood literalistically by orthodox Muslims, the story is told that the angels, having been created before Adam, were told to bow down and acknowledge in him God's supreme handiwork. Lucifer boggled at that proposal. He could not bring himself to obey God's command and so he and his fellow rebels were accordingly disciplined. (In such circumstances a Christian might well feel some sympathy with Lucifer!) Such an exaltation of humanity is contrary, of course, to the Christian tradition from the Letter to the Hebrews right on through St. Thomas and down to the present day. Angels, however conceived, are always assumed to be a higher order of being.

The consequences of such a view are important and interesting for modern thought, since they provide room for an outlook in which humanity, for all its grandeur and despite all its misery, is not merely a species (much less the final species) in the scheme of things but a stage in the evolutionary process. A human being is not a being who has "arrived"; he or she is a being on the way from lower forms of life to higher ones. Who knows what grander forms such higher life might take? The openness of the Nicene Creed to such possibilities makes it once again amenable to interpretations that do not at all conflict with the evolutionary model to which a modern scientific outlook in so many ways points.

The most fundamental question of all that we must face here is, What is the relationship between nature and God? Christian theologians have generally resisted every suggestion that might seem to identify them. In the long tradition of Christian mystical theology that has run alongside the "official" theological tradition, the tendency to bring God and nature too close for the liking of those in the mainstream of Christian orthodoxy has been notable. This tendency is detectable in the writings of the Pseudo-Dionysius, who flourished about the year 500 and who is generally accounted the fountainhead of all Christian mystical traditions. It is especially notable in the German school of mystics but is by no means absent from those in the Spanish, French, and English schools, despite the discreet language that mystics have used to veil what would have been taken as danger signs or worse. In oriental and other forms of nature-mysticism the identification of nature with God is generally open, undisguised and unselfconscious.

While identifying nature with God is plainly incompatible with what the Creed says and with what orthodox Christians, Jews, and Muslims, following biblical tradition, have always believed, we question the extreme position of those who make the created universe nothing definitely more than something God made as Shakespeare made *Hamlet* and Ibsen *Peer Gynt*. For that might mean that as Shakespeare and Ibsen might have written their plays differently, so God might have made the universe differently. Leibniz, in his proposal that ours is "the best of all possible worlds" (a notion much ridiculed by Voltaire), saw why any universe that God could choose to make otherwise would be even more absurd than the notion that the one we have is the best possible. The notion of God's standing so completely apart from the universe (as he does in Islam and in some mainstreams of Christian theology) certainly places an obstacle between science and theology today. Modern science is by no means incompatible with belief in God; but the notion that God willed the universe and chose one way of doing it rather than another, almost as one might choose French provincial furniture rather than Louis XV, does raise conundrums that perhaps need not be posed.

If what scientists observe and study is a universe that happens to be the way it is by an arbitrary fiat, then they would seem to be observing and studying shadow play, like the common people in Plato's "Allegory of the Cave." The pursuit of the sciences then becomes a study of a Western form of *maya:* an illusion made noble and exalted by reason of its divine origin, but still an illu-

sion. Instinctively, even the scientist who is most reverently disposed toward the idea of God tends to find that notion alien to all
his or her experience. To say, as Kepler is believed to have said as
he looked through the telescope, "O my God, I am thinking thy
thoughts after thee" (which Christians would generally applaud)
seems to say more. Thinker and thought are more intimately
connected than are the interior decorator and the furniture he or
she selects and even more close than are the dramatist and the play
he or she decides to write. The question is: "How much more inti-
mate may we account the relation between God and nature without infidelity to Christian orthodoxy?"

I would propose that Christian orthodoxy itself provides the
answer that best accords with the modern scientific outlook. God
does not make the universe "out of something" as does the divine
artist of Plato's *Timaeus;* he makes it "out of nothing," and we
have seen that this can only mean "nothing other than himself."
The universe must be then in some way an aspect of himself. "The
heavens declare the glory of God," as the Psalmist sings, not
because they are a masterpiece of his artistic skill as is da Vinci's
Mona Lisa; they declare God's glory because they reveal, however
obliquely, the divine Being.

Analogies are notoriously fraught with danger in such con-
texts, but I would venture the proposal that as my glance in your
direction manifests the "real me," so the universe manifests God
himself. Yet you might well mistake the significance of my look.
Suppose my look seemed stern or cold or even cruel (as does so
often nature), and you deduced that I must be such a person; you
might well be wrong. You *would* be wrong if I were, in fact, a
deeply loving person, whose love you could not readily understand
because of your too simplistic and superficial understanding of
love. Might not it be that, when we look at nature, we do see a
manifestation of God, however oblique, but cannot appreciate the
depth and the cost of the loving purpose that lies behind it in the
heart of God? Such an interpretation of Nicene orthodoxy seems to
me unobjectionable, and it is certainly much more amenable to
modern science than the suggestion that the universe around us
(together with space-time and all we can see and speculate about in
connection with what we see) has only an incidental or arbitrary
relationship with God.

My proposal would mean that God might be said to be theoretically knowable through nature as I might be said to be theoretically knowable through my glance. As my glance is, as we have seen, susceptible to radical misunderstanding, so the Being of God is not adequately unfolded or revealed to us through nature unless we have already experienced God more directly. I do not "see his blood upon the rose" or "in the stars the glory of his eyes" until I have seen God's love more intimately than it can be revealed in nature's public glance. According to the witness of the Nicene Creed, formulating what it takes to be the apostolic teaching, that is why God "became man" in the person of Jesus Christ: to reveal his love more intimately, more personally, than is possible through nature. To that central and peculiarly controversial question we must now turn as we throw on it such light as can be shed from the scientific knowledge of our day.

BEFORE the glorious throne of thy majesty, O Lord, and the awful judgment-seat of thy burning love, we thy people kneel with cherubim, seraphim, and archangels, worshipping, confessing, and praising thee, Lord of all, Father, Son, and Holy Spirit for ever.

—Chaldean liturgy

───── CHAPTER IV ─────

Uniqueness of Jesus Christ

And in one Lord Jesus Christ,
the only-begotten Son of God,
begotten of his Father before all worlds

"WHAT was will be again; what has been done will be done again; and there is nothing new under the sun" (Eccles. 1:9, New English Bible). These words of a Hebrew sage writing two centuries or more before the birth of Christ represent a view of wise men in every age and all over the world. They contain truth. This truth can be discerned by thoughtful people as soon as a civilization is sufficiently developed to allow people to think abstractly, reason logically, and look dispassionately at such historical records as are available to them.

To be able to reflect on history is a great step in the advancement of human knowledge and can be taken only long after people first attain the power of speech and use of language. When taken, that step intoxicates people with the insights it makes possible. To see, for example, that empires rise and fall, that people make the same mistakes decade after decade, that every generation of old people turns oversuspicious and every generation of young people thinks it is the first to have discovered sex, is the beginning of an important understanding of life. When people at last acquire the tools of rational thought, when they can see life as a panorama and can classify and analyze what they see, they have reached a new plateau in human development. They are no longer merely talking animals; they have become rational animals.

As with every step in any evolutionary process, however, becoming rational is not all gain. For the greater analytical power they have attained, people sacrifice much creative spontaneity. Human beings might wish they could fly, as wished the psalmist: "Oh for the wings of a dove" (Ps. 55:6, Jerusalem Bible). We might even wish we could swim like fish, without the hindrance of scuba gear. All these capacities we have sacrificed for something better than any bird or fish enjoys; nevertheless, we have lost something.

We need not, however, always lose all: we lack the keen scent that dogs and other lower animals possess, yet most of us have retained some olfactory capacity, along with our highly developed eyesight and other senses. The greatest geniuses in history have attained the highest powers of reasoning and abstract thought without sacrificing creativity. Too many people, however, have sacrificed all originality for only a modest supply of rational ability. In these days of computers that need only be programmed to do so many of our mathematical and logical problems for us, the loss of human creativity in exchange for such now commonplace skills may look somewhat pathetic, not to say tragic.

Almost the entire history of Western thought from Plato down to comparatively recent times was a history of rational thought. Of course there were exceptions, not least Plato himself, who is too great for any such label. In the thirteenth century Duns Scotus raised the question of novelty in his concept of "thisness"; but, till the Renaissance in the fifteenth and sixteenth centuries, the notion of originality and novelty was little discussed, and the failure to attend to it hampered and delayed the development of modern scientific investigations. Today even notably able minds are often still in the grip of an almost exclusively rationalist approach to reality. This rationalist approach, which first enabled people to see the truth in the notion of a cyclic element in history, tends to make them proceed to the conclusion, which that Hebrew sage also seems to have reached, that all history is cyclic.

Taken strictly, the view that there is nothing new under the sun is not supported in modern scientific thought. It is especially unsupported in what we have learned of the evolutionary principle in biology. The emergence of even the most primitive forms of life introduces a startling novelty on a planet where living things did not previously exist. The emergence of mind is another and equally breathtaking novelty. That "history repeats itself" is conspicuously a half-truth, or, more precisely, a half-truism; for it is no less obvious that history never repeats itself. I might return to my birthplace with clocklike regularity every ten years of my life, each time celebrating my birthday with exactly the same ritual; but of course not only would each celebration not be an exact replica of the previous one; I would not be at all the same person on my thirtieth birthday that I had been on my twentieth; nor would I have been the same on my twentieth as on my tenth. History is strictly unrepeatable. Even if I were to be reincarnated along with my own parents, reborn in the same room of the same hospital, and educated at the same school, history would not be repeating itself; because my having already lived before, I would not be exactly the same person.

These elementary reflections on the intractable philosophical problem of novelty relate in a fascinating way to the Christian claim that the Christ-event in human history is unique. The claim is not that Jesus Christ is unique: every human being is unique, each having his or her unique fingerprints and vocal peculiarities, for example. The claim is that, in the antique language of the Creed, Jesus Christ is "the only-begotten Son of God," so that with him a new era was begun and the entire course of human history was changed and transmogrified. The claim to novelty is not merely a claim that Jesus is greater than Plato or Gautama, as one might allege that bass is superior to salmon or that Shakespeare is better than Cervantes.

The orthodox Christian claim, grounded in what the Nicene Creed expresses in its fourth-century terms, is that Jesus Christ led the greatest of all evolutionary developments in human history (some would prefer to say cosmic history), introducing a new age, an age that will in turn give place to another at his Second Coming. Jesus Christ, Christians claim, was able to do this because his status is different from that of every other human being, even those most deeply touched by the Spirit of God. It is not that there is no one else entirely like him; there is no one else entirely like you or like me either. It is, rather, that there is no other who is both wholly divine and wholly human.

The claim is indeed staggering, the more so when we begin

to work out its implicates. For instance, to be human he had to enter human history at a certain place (traditionally Bethlehem) and at a certain time, with all the particularity inseparable from the finitude in which he chose to imprison himself for the working out of God's amazing love. This "scandal of particularity" is what has perhaps more than anything else troubled thoughtful people, not least philosophers trained in rationalist thinking.

Many years ago, just before Sputnik, I was walking on Blackford Hill, Edinburgh, with Norman Kemp Smith, whom I had for long known and venerated. He was by then elderly and regarded by many as the doyen of British philosophers. He is still internationally acclaimed for his work on Kant. Even in his eighties he had kept up a lively interest in the most significant new developments in philosophy and science. As we walked, he had been talking to me of the importance for philosophy of Einstein's work. As was often his habit, he lapsed into a silence that continued for at least a hundred yards of slow walking. Then suddenly he turned to me and, seeming to change the subject completely, he remarked: "I have no difficulty with the idea of God, but I do with that of Christ: one time, one place. Very difficult."

The sudden break in the silence, and then in the conversational stream, jolted me at the time. His views on Christianity came as no surprise to me. What surprised me was, rather, that he should have alluded to it at all, especially in such a disconnected way, after talking about Einstein. It was analogous to one's talking about exploring the Arctic and someone else's saying that he had nothing against music but did not like Mozart. Only much later did I perceive an odd connection: the sudden break, the discontinuity in the conversation, is not without parallels in the evolution of life, and it is precisely what Christian orthodoxy affirms about "the mystery of the Incarnation."

Norman Kemp Smith was voicing a very widespread feeling about Christianity. The "scandal of particularity," as Christians often call it, is still a stumbling block now, as it was to Paul's hearers. It is now, however, usually a stumbling block for a different reason from theirs, as we shall presently see.

Since a knowledge of the Orient and of "other major religions of the world" was opened up to the West, which did not take place till little more than a century ago, in any form definite and serious enough to affect even the vanguard of Western scholarship, the uniqueness claimed for Christ has become, for many, more than they can swallow. If we examine the nature of the claim, we have a further difficulty. Are Christians saying that Jesus Christ is Lord of all human beings on this planet and Redeemer of all of them who accept him as their Saviour and do his will? Or are we to understand that the realm of his lordship extends over the whole universe, so as to include, say, Martians, if there are any, and the inhabitants of galaxies in which there must surely be some planets with intelligent life? If so, does that mean that as soon as we get radio signals from them, Christians ought immediately to inquire whether they know that their Lord and Saviour came to *our* planet to save them, and, if they confess ignorance, should not Christian missionaries then collect money at once to make possible the journey to bring the gospel to them, if the evangelical enterprise cannot be conducted entirely by signals? Or must we recognize that there may be another Christ for Mars whom orthodox Martians acclaim True God and True Martian?

Then again, might we have to say that Christ's coming was only for the known world at the time and place and in the culture in which Jesus lived, a world that consisted chiefly of the Mediterranean basin and some lands that we now call the Middle East? In this case we might well point to lands such as India and China (where great civilizations flourished when Europe, after the fall of Rome, was a backwater, not to say a disaster area), and say that, when apostles of the Christian Way spoke of "the world," they could have meant just that. We might then go on to propose that God's intention was to provide a full and final revelation of himself for that little world, including us whose culture and civilization were cradled in it, but that he no more intended Christ for China than for Mars or that planet in outer space that may in the future send us signals.

Our contemporary preoccupation with outer space and our natural concern for the possibility, if not the probability, of extraterrestrial life, brings all such questions into focus. We are talking of such staggering distances that even with light travelling at 186,000 miles a second, a signal from astronomers on a planet two thousand light years away might have been sent before Jesus was born on earth. It is difficult for us not to see something very parochial in the outlook of the earnest Christian missionaries, Catholic and Protestant, Lutheran and Anglican, Methodist and Baptist, who went to India and China and Japan to convert the inhabitants to the Christian faith. Yet what else could they have done if they believed the gospel with its clear command to go forth and teach all nations?

Moreover, even as the missionaries were thus engaged, some people in intellectualist circles in England were suggesting that Jesus had been "mere man," while the people in India, the object of the missionaries' zeal, were so accustomed to the notion of periodic incarnations (*avatars*) of the gods that, in their opinion, one *avatar* more or less could not justify all the fuss the missionaries were making. India is an an ancient land, habituated to religious ideas long before they had confronted the Mediterranean world in Paul's preaching. India has been for centuries a sophisticated clearinghouse for such ideas, as England and America have become, in the last two hundred years, clearinghouses for economic ones. By the time of Jesus, however, that Mediterranean world had indeed become such a clearinghouse for religious ideas. It was by any standards as sophisticated and creative about them as it was, by our current standards, uncreative and unsophisticated about economics and technology. Had it been otherwise, people would hardly have come to hear what Paul and others had to say, even if (in many cases) only to reject it.

The apostolic proclamation would have generally struck them as absurd, not because (as is the situation among those who applaud contemporary conclusions such as those fostered by some of the authors of books such as *The Myth of God Incarnate*) the idea of a god's descent from heaven would have seemed ridiculous (when in fact it would have seemed to them commonplace in religious lore), but, rather, because the Christians were saying something far more special than that. They were saying, in their Jewish way, that there is only one God, and they were then going on to identify him with an obscure Jewish rabbi who had been crucified, presumably for some political shenanigans. They were saying that Jesus was not only "the Christ," the Anointed One, the long-expected Messiah of his people (a very special, not to say parochial people at that), but also the Son of God, the God whom the Jews claimed to be the one, the only God. "Jesus," the apostles of the

Christian Way were saying, "is *the only Son of the only God.*"
The presuppositions of the typical skeptic among Paul's hearers
and of the average contemporary reader who concludes that Jesus
was "only a man" are radically different.

We have already seen that the Nicene Creed is at more than
one point open to a variety of interpretations. In one case especially (the almightiness of God), we have noticed how the removal
of a traditional misunderstanding can both dispel obscurity and
enrich our conception of the grandeur we attribute to God. Now,
however, we face an affirmation of the uniqueness of Jesus Christ
that seems much less open to such optional interpretations. He is
not merely said to be divine, as is every *avatar* in every polytheis-
tic mythology, oriental or occidental. Nor is he merely said to be a
child of the one True God as was everyone among the people of
Israel then as now, and as all we Christians claim to be (sons if
male, daughters if female); he is uncompromisingly acclaimed
"the only-begotten Son of God."

This affirmation, which is behind what is now traditionally
called in theological shorthand "the divinity of Christ," has been
from an early point in Christian history at the core of orthodoxy.
It has been so both in the Eastern Church and in the Western, both
among Anglicans and among Lutherans, both in Roman Catholic
tradition and in the classic Reformation heritage. It is part of that
"scandal of particularity" to which we have already alluded. Those
who, in Unitarian and other such fashion, have denied it have been
traditionally accounted heretics *par excellence*, and their denial
has been customarily recognized as the most direct and succinct
way of saying: "I am not a Christian, though with Jews and
Muslims I recognize Jesus to have been a notable prophet."

When Coleridge, who was given to inventing neologisms,
coined the word *humanism* for the first time in English in or about
1834, he was referring specifically to the theological opinion of
those who denied "the divinity of Christ." Humanism has since
come to have, of course, a wide variety of meanings and would
hardly ever be understood today in that narrow sense; but its
emergence in that sense in comparatively recent times in the
English-speaking world reminds us of how the denial of Christ's
divinity has been traditionally regarded.

Those who, at various times in the history of Christian

thought, denied the divinity of Christ, inevitably did so without the finely honed tools of modern scholarship. They usually did it simplistically, having started out with a literalistic understanding of the Gospels. Developments in historiography and in New Testament scholarship since the middle of the last century have taught thoughtful Christians the need to be much more critical of any literalistic interpretation of the classic documents of their faith than were, for example, most of their nineteenth-century forefathers. Modern biblical scholars also know, however, that in both ancient and medieval times the learned generally tended to read the Bible, as has been noted earlier, allegorically rather than literalistically, indeed sometimes extravagantly so. The application of modern methods of literary criticism to the biblical literature has given us a perspective not available to scholars in the past, to people, for example, in the age of Kierkegaard and the early Newman. We also know today, as people did not generally know then, how extremely limited is our knowledge of the historical Jesus.

We know, too, better than did our forefathers, the background of the New Testament and how people conceptualized religious ideas in the time of Christ. What some modern scholars have sometimes failed to take seriously is the possibility that the *presuppositions* of the ancients about religion might have been more enlightened and more methodologically useful than the ones biblical scholars today are generally trained to have. To that we shall return.

Even in the early part of the present century scholars such as Adolf Deissmann were shedding much light on that New Testament background. Other scholars were seeing too that it was not just a case of unearthing more and more manuscript fragments from Egypt and elsewhere and using them for checking the accuracy of our knowledge of New Testament beginnings, but a case of getting into the mood of the ancient world and the *Sitz im Leben* as the Germans call it, as a preliminary to understanding anything we unearth.

A simple example can serve to illustrate this point. When I talk about a day's journey, you will generally suppose that I had covered perhaps 400 miles by car or 4000 miles by air, but of course to people who journey by donkey or camel or on foot the phrase means something extremely different. When such differences are multiplied many times, the distance between our thought and that of, say, the writers of the New Testament literature is so great as to be a serious obstacle. For it is not only that it engenders misunderstanding about facts and events. That might matter comparatively little. But it also engenders misunderstanding about the motivations, the attitudes, behind the facts and events. What is crucial for any interpretation of the Bible, then, is a recognition of the differences in modes of conceptualizing and especially in presupposition.

In 1935 H. J. Cadbury, a noted biblical scholar at Harvard, published *The Peril of Modernizing Jesus.* It was rightly influential. Having read accounts of the life of Jesus, such as one that depicted a modern suburban villa with several upstairs bedrooms, he concluded that if one could be so wrong about the physical details of life in Palestine in the time of Jesus, how much more profoundly wrong would one be likely to be about what was going on inside the heads of people of that age, their mental outlook and their ideological presuppositions. Scholars today are well aware of all this; yet they are not always by any means equally aware of the vigor and potency of their own presuppositions or of the sometimes astoundingly uncritical attitude they bring to bear on them.

In 1947 the discovery of the Qumran documents ushered in a new era of illumination of New Testament background. More and more, the influence of Gnostic and similar outlooks was being discerned behind the written words of the New Testament as it has come down to us. Yet the discovery of the Qumran documents and of the Nag Hammadi Library (more recently also available in English translation) has done little to shake the confidence of biblical scholars in the superiority of the presuppositions of our day over those of the first century *in all respects.* They are working with analytical tools that have served well in certain disciplines and for certain limited purposes; but one could no more advance radically using only such tools than could Max Planck have advanced from the old physics to the quanta using strictly positivistic and analytical methods. The implications of Planck's experience for our purpose are tremendous.

When we ask whether the presuppositions of today are always the ones justified by modern science, we cannot by any means give an unequivocal yes. Of course it seems obvious in many domains, but is it inevitably and universally the case? True, nobody in New Testament times knew how to do history as modern historians expect it to be done, and as generally seems to us a good way, if not the only way, to do it. The cosmology of writers of that time has been shown over and over again to have been outmoded. They were far behind us in their knowledge of physics and chemistry and they were grossly primitive in their biology. Yet a man may be the most competent engineer in the world and be a simpleton in linguistics, while another may have the literary creativity of a Joyce or a Proust and be incapable of fixing a leaky faucet. Indeed, it often happens that the one is foolishly contemptuous of the other.

A striking example of the inability or unwillingness of some modern scholars to criticize their own presuppositions and to question the prejudices of our age is provided by one of the contributors to the symposium[1] to which I have alluded. Michael Goulder, in his account of what he calls a Samaritan and a Galilean theology, shows that the Samaritan one has been saturated with Gnostic ways of thought. While acknowledging that "historical study does not disprove divine activity," he goes on at once to add, "it just renders the old inspirational model implausible." He has detected errors in what both the Samaritans and the Galileans have said and feels able to say of the traditional doctrine of the Incarnation "that it is not believable today, and that our generation is called to formulate its christology anew." He concludes that "the incarnational speculations introduced into the church by Simon Magus and his fellow Samaritans seem to me entirely dispensable."

Whether or not we accept the particular historical analysis of this author (another in the symposium, Frances Young, rightly expresses her dissatisfaction with it), I suggest that we ought to see in it a typical example of how modern scholars often arbitrarily renounce traditional orthodoxy *simply* because it reflects attitudes of mind that are alien to ones prevailing in some areas of inquiry today. I am not concerned with the historical grounds the author adduces, which happen to be questionable, but with the readiness with which he repudiates Nicene orthodoxy only because of its not

1. John Hick, ed., *The Myth of God Incarnate* (Philadelphia: Westminster Press, 1977).

having presuppositions that conform to a prevailing fashion among textual scholars and analytical philosophers.

Reluctance to try to understand religious ideas as they emerge phenomenologically is so striking in academic circles in the English-speaking world that some observers have gone so far as to suggest that there may be something in the English temper that inhibits or obscures such understanding! Be that as it may, one cannot but notice an obtuseness about religious experience not ordinarily expected in men of such intellectual training and ability.

The relevance of such reflections to our present theme is not difficult to show. Apart from the presuppositions of the New Testament writers, which are now more and more recognized to have a Gnostic background, the New Testatment is so unintelligible that what should really astonish us is that anybody without the kind of experience that leads to a Gnostic view of life should ever have given it any credence at all. I suspect that in fact no one has ever really believed the Christian message without some experience, however vague, akin to that of the people in the time of Jesus. That type of experience is certainly not reducible to our everyday experience of the external world. The kind of statements now confronting us in those articles of the Nicene Creed that relate to belief in "the divinity of Christ" cannot but seem nonsensical till one takes seriously ideas such as those to which modern parapsychology and similar types of scientific inquiry lead. In the past, all "official" theology in the Church tended to discountenance and indeed discredit such theories as "occultist" or "magical." Yet without the recognition of a realm of psychic realities not discernible as are trees and waterfalls or even frowns and smiles, the traditional picture of Jesus Christ and his relation to us and to God is not simply incredible; it is nonsensical. So whatever we propose to do with it, we must, if we wish first to understand it, see it from the standpoint of those who were aware of and were habitually confronted by such a realm.

Taking such notions seriously today is surely much easier than it would have been at, say, the beginning of last century. For no ordinarily openminded person today can fail to recognize the presence among us of at least some psychic phenomena, such as telepathy and hypnotism, which were not known then except in underground circles. During the past century or so, the societies for psychical research in both America and England have patiently examined psychic phenomena till no one today can deny that there is at least "something in them" that cannot be explained in terms of physics and other traditional "natural" sciences. Since there is no other way of making any sense at all of the Gospel accounts of Jesus on which Nicene orthodoxy rests, we must surely take such notions very seriously indeed. Otherwise we cannot but be forced into some sort of theological or exegetical legerdemain to keep up a pretense of intelligibility.

The affirmation we are now looking at is the first of four that relate to the traditional doctrine of the Incarnation. It is the end-point, however, in a metaphysical construction arising from an interpretation of what the first-century Christians experienced. To anyone familiar with what are nowadays called "psychic" modes of experience, examples saturate the Gospels. In Mark, for instance, generally accounted the most "matter-of-fact" account of the life of Jesus, we have the story of a woman who, plagued by a hemorrhage for twelve years, came up to Jesus in a crowd and touched his clothes in the belief that by so doing she would be cured. The holiness and spiritual strength she perceived in him would permeate even the clothes he wore. That could be taken, as it generally is taken, to reflect the persistence of old, primitive, "magical" superstition. If so, the superstition would have to be attributed also to Jesus, for he is immediately aware that "virtue" (*dynamis*, power) has gone out of him. He turns round, asking who touched him. The resurrection narratives also abound in instances that exhibit "psychic" awareness.

The story in Acts of Paul's conversion is startling. Paul never saw Jesus in the flesh. He first encountered him in a vision, followed by a light so powerful that he is blinded by it for several days. Eventually, scales fall from his eyes, he rises, is baptized, takes some food, and feels strong again. We may note in passing that in the early days of the Church, baptism was sometimes called *phōtismos*, enlightenment. Surely we cannot avoid noting the strikingly "psychic" character of the account. It has parallels, indeed, in the experiences of mystics and visionaries all over the world and of very diverse backgrounds, so that we are forced to conclude either that (1) such experiences are hallucinations, the result of mental disturbance, or (2) they arise from the encounter of realities in a psychic realm that are not visible or audible as is the color of your hair or the pitch of your voice. We must learn to appreciate that it is upon experiences such as these that the whole development of the doctrine of "the divinity of Christ" rests. John, the "light-in-darkness" evangelist, is not by any means alone in his witness to that sort of development.

The Gospels abound also in references by Jesus himself to his special knowledge of "the Father." He is hailed at his baptism as God's "beloved" Son, which is almost as peculiar and distinctive as "only-begotten." The uniqueness attributed to Jesus is not merely the uniqueness of a messiah. He claims an affinity with God that is unique. The New Testament writers and early Fathers of the Church, in their efforts to express that affinity, had to resort to the philosophical constructs of their day, such as the notion of "substance," which we will consider in the next chapter; but the testimony they give us shows that while they were well accustomed to thinking in "psychic" terms and had seen glimmerings of the manifestation of divine Being in various holy men and women, they were recognizing in Jesus the presence of the divine energy *at its source*. We must now see how modern scientific views of matter and light can help us to understand better the stupendous claim the New Testament writers make.

O Lord Jesus Christ, who hast said thou art the way, the truth, and the life; suffer us not at any time to stray from thee, who art the way; nor to distrust thy promises, who art the truth; nor to rest in anything other than thee, who art the life; beyond which there is nothing to be desired in heaven or on earth; for thy Name's sake. Amen

—Erasmus
(sixteenth century)

-------CHAPTER V-------

Light of Light

God of God, Light of Light,
very God of very God;
begotten, not made, being of one substance with the Father,
by whom all things were made

WHEN Jesus asked the disciples (Matt. 16:13ff.) who people said that he was, they told him that some thought he was Elijah, others Jeremiah, and so forth. That a prophet should be the reincarnation of a holy man of old was plainly within the ambit of popular thought. Peter, however, according to Matthew's account (16:16), acknowledges that Jesus is "the Christ, the Son of the living God," and receives the approval of Jesus, who tells him that this is something he could not have discovered through any ordinary study or from any standard scholarly inquiry but only through God himself, whom Jesus here as elsewhere calls "my Father."

The phrases "very God of very God, begotten not made, being of one substance with the Father," were added to earlier formulations of Christian belief specifically to deny what the followers of Arius were saying. They were saying that while they accepted the biblical view, to which Greek philosophy also pointed, that God is One, they understood Jesus to have been created by God and therefore, however great a creature, still on this side of the infinite gulf between God and his created universe. From the use of the metaphor "Father and Son," they argued plausibly that sonship implies creation: how could one who is coeternal with the Father be called "Son"? We must be careful not to identify the

41

views of Arius with those of people today who deny "the divinity of Christ." The Arians did see Christ as unique. They could even call him divine in the general sense in which the term *theos* was used in the Greek-speaking world, though not in the special sense of the One God who is absolute and absolutely separated from all creation by the infinite abyss that in biblical thought must always lie between He-Who-Creates and that-which-is-created. In the Arian view Christ could be called "without peer in creation" and divine in that vague sense familiar both in philosophical discussion and popular usage.

The Arian view was, then, a subtle one that emerged in an intellectual climate in which people were trying to marry classical Hebrew thought about God with remnants of a polytheism that was still ideologically near to the thought of even the most thoughtful Gentiles. The Church, in rejecting Arianism, used a concept prominent in Aristotelian thought and familiar in Greek philosophical discussion generally: *ousia*, substance, essence. It was a technical term that provoked controversy even in the fourth century in the context in which it was used to repudiate the Arian position; much later it was to be the focus of bitter controversy, especially in the medieval Roman doctrine of transubstantiation in the Mass, according to which the bread and wine change their "substance" while retaining the "accidents" that make them look and taste like bread and wine: a thoroughly Aristotelian mode of conceptualizing. Now that the concept of "substance" has been for long entirely discarded in contemporary thought as entailing a useless and/or meaningless distinction, its use in the Creed must be regarded today as an archaic survival. Nevertheless, what it has intended from the first to affirm is no less important today than when it was first formulated.

What it affirms is doubtless a mystical notion, one that presupposes that the Christian Way entails relationships to God and the Christian community such as Paul had in mind in talking of Christ as the Head of the Body and in talking of the Christian as being "in" Christ. These are plainly metaphors that reflect a very special, mystical understanding of the Christian experience. The Nicene Creed presupposes some such experience. So when it asserts that Christ is "of one substance" with God, it recognizes that the Christian is right in relating himself to Christ exactly as he would relate himself to God. Christian experience is that God has given *himself* in Christ; it is *not* that in an exceptionally great and holy fellow creature we are enabled to see more of God than we do in ourselves. We can appreciate the force of the distinction only when we appreciate the nature of the gulf between Creator and creature. The Creed is affirming that God has bridged the gulf by giving himself. The concept is a very mystical one indeed, and traditional defenses of orthodoxy have too often neglected to insist on this fact. All religious truths must always be expressed in mythological language, and of course the linguistic models used in the fourth century are sure to be very different from those we would be likely to use today; nevertheless, we must be on that very account especially careful not to traduce the meaning under pretext of translating the language.

Moreover, the notion that an incarnational understanding of the fundamental message of Christianity is less scientific than a nonincarnational one is entirely unwarranted. Not only is the latter interpretation no more plausible in the light of current scientific methods and knowledge; it is even more absurd, since it entails our still calling Jesus in some sense Lord and Saviour when he is taken to be only a fellow creature, a notion which is surely a romantic hero-worship, not to say idolatry. The ancient *mythos* about the appearance of the gods in human form comes in many ludicrous guises; but those guises are no more ludicrous than modern *mythoi* in which contemporary folk heroes are acclaimed, not to say deified.

We are not justified, however, in deducing from that either (1) that we should not respect and honor distinguished men and women of our time, or (2) that we should not take seriously the concept that God's fullest revelation of himself to us might take the form of an encampment among us in the Person of Jesus Christ. In short, if we are open to the concept of God's unfolding of himself to us through words or pictures, the notion of his unfolding himself by sharing our human condition must surely seem apposite. And once we do that, we cannot have much difficulty in recognizing the need to say, specifically and emphatically, as does the Nicene Creed in its fourth-century way, that Jesus is *not* a creature like the rest of us but the Eternal One outpouring himself.

The Nicene Creed calls Jesus Christ "Light of Light." The

metaphor of light is extremely ancient as a means of expressing the
notion of intelligence, contradistinguished from physical "substance" or "matter." Augustine writes of having turned his mind
inside itself and of finding there "above" his own mind "the in-
communicable light" of God. This metaphor, like many others,
was even more apt than the ancients could have known. For we
have now learned more of the peculiar role of light in the universe.
As has been already hinted, the story of the development of
theories about light is perhaps the most exciting in the history of
physics; nor, surely, has it all been told yet.

The aim of the older theories was to reduce matter to a mere
agglomeration of indivisible elementary particles all definitely
localized in space. The motion of electrons within atoms, however,
could not be made to obey the laws of classical mechanics. The
revolution in physics has led to a recognition that reality cannot be
interpreted in terms of continuity only: some individual entities
must be discerned within the continuity; yet these entities are not
describable as simply "discontinuous" for they have extension and
they are continually reacting on one another. While there are
plainly several ways in which the result of such findings could be
interpreted, the models to which modern physics point all suggest
a universe in which energy is the key concept.

Light stands in a very special relation to energy. It is part of
the restlessness in the microcosmic world that is the focus of so
much of modern scientific research. Even where atoms seem to be
absent, as in "empty" interstellar space, light rays are present,
moving in many directions. Many are the paradoxes relating to
light. For instance, light plus light does not necessarily give more
light but may, under some circumstances, produce darkness. The
light we can see represents only a small fraction of the light that is
"at work" in the universe.

The peculiarity of the nature and behavior of light suggests
that the nature of the universe is such that we need no longer think
in terms of the dualism of mind and matter as it is traditionally
presented to us in classical Western philosophy. God is not to be
seen as different "in essence" from everything else (i.e., in biblical
terms, his "creation"); nor is my mind so radically different from
my body as Descartes and others thought. Yet for all that, we
cannot go on to think of everything as evenly "spread out" and all

of "one stuff" as did the old materialists. On the contrary, physicists speak today of energy and mass. Energy is the capacity to do work, by which is meant the moving of a body against the action of some force, as when we lift a heavy weight or build and fly an airplane, working in both instances against the law of gravity. We are only too well aware of what can be done, for good or ill, to obtain energy by tampering with the atomic nucleus.

In the light of modern physics, the notion that a "place" might be opened up for the source of energy to act in a special, even unique way, to make that fount uniquely available to us, is, to say the least, far more plausible than it was when "classical" physics prevailed. Energy is power. Hitherto (one might suggest) we had seen power mainly in seeing it abused; but now at this "place," this "clearance," we may say that Christ (the "Light of the world") opens up the outpouring of the energy of which he is the source. So, then, the old metaphor that he is "Light of Light" as he is "God of God" is singularly apposite.

My main point here is that such ways of thinking are not at all so alien to modern scientific thought as some modern biblical scholars and theologians would have us believe. They are alien only to special presuppositions held by these scholars and theologians, which derive virtually nothing from the science of today but, rather, from the prejudices of some scientists of yesterday, when mechanistic models of the universe made such prejudices more excusable.

We cannot too often remind ourselves that the models and metaphors used by the early Fathers and in the early creeds are "open" ones. They were not devised to confine us to one narrow way of thinking. In using the metaphor of "shepherd" for God, the psalmist did not intend to require people to go back to a pastoral rather than an urban life in order to understand the nature of God. He used it no doubt because it came readily to mind. We need only know how a shepherd relates to his sheep to understand what the psalmist is asserting: God's compassion and care for us. He is not purporting to tell us all the characteristics of God. He is concentrating on this particular one. We can do with the metaphor what we will, provided that we have first grasped the general intention of the author: God deals with us, not like a drill sergeant, but more like a shepherd. So in using the old metaphysical metaphor of "substance" and the physical metaphor of "light," the Nicene Creed is asserting that whatever Christ is, he is not a creature. It happens, however, that, from a modern standpoint, "substance" is an outmoded metaphor, while "light" is a better one for us than the ancient Fathers could possibly have predicted.

From the time of Aristotle, space has been understood in Western philosophy as a finite receptacle into which could be put, obviously, only finite "things." The Christian Fathers in the early Church did not like this notion; but with the rediscovery of Aristotle in the twelfth century, when his system became the "secular" challenge (as we might say) to the Latin Church, it affected the scholastic thought of the Middle Ages. For Aristotle was to the great Christian scholars (Thomas Aquinas and others) what "science" has been to theologians during the past two or three centuries: human knowledge that had to be reckoned with in formulating a statement of Christian faith. Since the Aristotelian concept of space as a finite receptacle did not fit the Church's central belief in the Incarnation, a peculiar kind of dualism emerged that has haunted Christian thought ever since: the notion of two orders, one natural and the other supernatural, operating independently in an "upstairs-downstairs" arrangement.

Contemporary thought, which encourages the use of a different model in which we talk of dimensions rather than levels or floors, is in fact much closer to the intellectual climate of the early Church. The "spiritual" and the "carnal" are not to be thought of as two worlds but, rather, as two dimensions, interpenetrating each other as do energy and mass. With the "upstairs-downstairs" model, the notion of an incarnation of the divine cannot but seem artificial, even ridiculous. The dimensional model does not make it less of an intellectual surprise. (Nothing could do that, for the Incarnation is God's surprise for us.) But it does make the surprise more intelligible and therefore easier to appreciate by those spiritually prepared to apprehend it, who, as John says, are "born not of blood nor of the will of the flesh nor of the will of man, but of God."

If, as has been earlier suggested as a viable interpretation of Nicene orthodoxy, God is eternally creating and therefore eternally impinging on the universe that is his creation, the notion that he should enter into it in a peculiar way at a particular time and place, and for a special purpose, is not at all unthinkable, astonishing though it must always be.

What Nicene orthodoxy does not permit is the explaining away of the doctrine of the Incarnation by saying that Christ is either merely a "God-like" creature or a divine lamp carried from "upstairs" to "downstairs." No, God himself was in Christ. The divine light shone in Christ in its fulness. It shone as never before on earth. To avoid any diminishment of this affirmation, any modification that might be adopted to fit the mood or fashion of any age or generation, anywhere or at any time, the Creed affirms that Jesus Christ is "God of God, Light of Light."

Twentieth-century science is filled with the unexpected, such as tunneling effects created when electrons penetrate barriers that are accounted impenetrable, waves of electrons perceived before they are generated, and particles (tachyons) that travel faster than light. That whole spectrum of the unexpected paves the way for taking a new view and making a much more serious estimate of the significance of the notion of the Incarnation of God in time. In contrast to the world of the older physics, which was a world of "facts," the world of contemporary science is much more a world of potentialities. In short, with our conception of the universe, we are far more open than were earlier generations to the notion of personal factors interacting with what was formerly thought of as impersonal nature. Perception can no longer be seen as merely the apprehension of realms of "matter" and "life" that the human mind is somehow able to apprehend because it has been mysteriously endowed with the capacity to do so. We can no longer think of mind as locked in an observation box looking out at non-mind, any more than we can think in terms of a spiritual reality and a material reality with special channels and a communications system enabling contact to be made in specific instances. The world confronting scientists today is not at all like that.

That does not mean that modern physics leads us even a step nearer the notion of the Incarnation as it is so emphatically proclaimed in the Creed. Modern science does not necessarily lead us even to the interpretation that there is a God such as is presupposed in the earlier articles of the Creed before the question of Christ is broached at all. It can make people more open to that interpretation, however, and once that interpretation has been made, the affirmation that Jesus Christ is the embodying of God in human flesh is by no means as unthinkable as it was on the old presuppositions of a mechanistic physics.

To talk, then, as do some theologians today, of whether or not the doctrine of the Incarnation is "logically coherent" is surely to ask the wrong kind of question. It is not a question of logic. If it were a question of logic, the doctrine could never have been formulated as it was. In formulating it, the Nicene Fathers were saying, in effect, that this is something to which logic could never possibly lead us and that, if it could, there would be no need to say it the way it was said. What twentieth-century scientific thought does is to help to remove certain obstacles to the doctrine's apprehension, obstacles that had been artificially placed there by outmoded forms of science.

ALMIGHTY and everlasting God, the brightness of faithful souls, who didst bring the peoples to thy light and make known unto them him who is the true Light and the bright and morning star, fill, we beseech thee, the world with thy glory, and by the radiance of thy Light show thyself unto all nations; through Jesus Christ our Lord.

—Gregorian Sacramentary
(sixth century)

CHAPTER VI

Our Salvation

*Who for us men and for our salvation
came down from heaven*

THE least important phrase in the Nicene Creed is "came down from heaven." Some people today make a great fuss about that notion, pointing to it as representing an outmoded cosmology, in which the earth is conceived as a vast saucer with the sky above it, covering it as would an inverted bowl, above which is situated God's throne. That was indeed one of the cosmologies of the ancient world, though not the only one, and the figure of speech used was certainly a natural way for the ancients to express the entry of God into humanity in the Person of Jesus Christ: a belief at the core of Nicene faith. It would have been in any case, however, a natural way for the authors of the Nicene Creed to express what they needed to say. Such a figure of speech did not at all limit them to thinking in terms of a descent from a localized heaven "up there" to a flat earth "down here." In their own way the ancients could not but have seen beyond any fashionable cosmology of the day when they used this figure of speech, for it pertains to the human condition itself.

Deeply embedded in all human thought and language is the notion that whatever is good is "up" and whatever is bad is "down." We habitually talk of "lofty" ideals and "high" principles as we also speak of "base" actions and "low" conduct. In doing so, we do not in any way depend on the archaic astronomy of this or that age or civilization, nor do we need to rely on any quaint survival of such outmoded conceptions of the universe.

The up-down figure of speech reflects the organization of our own bodies. The highest part of our extraordinarily complex human body is the human brain, which contains more than twelve billion nerve cells with some 1,000,000,000,000,000,000,000,000 potential "telephone connections," all within the three pounds of pinkish-gray tissue contained in the skull of each one of us. The higher intellectual processes, such as reading and writing, are centered in the cerebrum, the physically uppermost part of the brain, under which are several "sub-brains," which direct the merely life-sustaining functions that we have in common with other animals. These animal functions, notably our breathing and our digestion of food and drink, are performed in the lower parts of our physical structure. In a half-jocose but highly apposite way, we often refer to the part of the body on which we sit as our "bottom." It is at this level that are performed our functions of elimination (urinary and defecatory) as well as that of copulation. These functions, excretory and genital, are obviously essential, the former to our fundamental well-being, the latter to the survival of the human race. With such an arrangement, however, a human being, especially a highly developed one, cannot but find it natural to use figures of speech rooted in the notion that all that is preeminently valuable and specifically human is "up," while all that is common to all animals, however healthy or necessary, is "down."

True, it is possible that, if we were to rewrite the Nicene Creed, we might prefer to say that Jesus Christ came "from the deep core of all things, which is God the Father Almighty," or to use some other such metaphor instead of the "heavenly" one. The latter, however, is not only deeply rooted in our experience of our own bodies, but it also pervades Scripture, being found not least in the words attributed to Jesus himself: "our Father in heaven" and "your heavenly Father," for instance. Why should we boggle at such figurative expressions that are both natural and hallowed by long and loving use?

When I exclaim, "Come see the moon—look, it's right up there above the Capitol," not even the most pedantic astronomer berates me for such an outmoded way of talking. No one hastens to tell me that neither the sun nor the moon is really "up" and that this has been known to astronomers for hundreds of years. Why, then, should one have to endure tedious instruction to the effect that God could not "come down from heaven," if only because there is no heaven "up there" since there is no "up there" for either a heaven or anything else to be? Yet the notions of the "up-there-ness" of heaven and of God's being located there are remarkably ingrained in the minds of many, as is shown by the extraordinary popularity of Bishop Robinson's little book *Honest to God,* as well as by the jejune remark of the Soviet cosmonaut who informed the world that he had been up there in space and had not come across God in any of his travels.

So let us concentrate on the rest of the words before us in this chapter: "who for us men and for our salvation." On the one hand, these words must concern, most profoundly, every intelligent and sensitive human being, for they raise a group of questions that everyone asks in one way or another, such as "What is the meaning of life?" "Why am I here?" "Whither am I bound?" and even the question put by Paul's jailer, "What must I do to be saved?" (Acts 16:30). On the other hand, the question "Are you saved?" plainly elicits the parry, "Saved from what?"

This last question is by no means necessarily flippant. Doctor Johnson once expressed the fear that he might be damned. His host, Doctor Adams, asked the proper, not to say obvious, question, "What do you mean by 'damned'?" At this Doctor Johnson, according to his biographer, retorted in a loud and passionate voice, "Sent to hell, Sir, and punished everlastingly." No doubt many have understood *salvation* to mean being saved from precisely that fate. We shall be in a better position toward the end of this book to consider the meaning of "heaven" and "hell" when we discuss what Christian theologians call "Last Things," but for the present let us glance at some ways that *salvation* might well be interpreted.

The horrific doctrine of hell has not been universally held by Christians, though it has certainly played a dominant role in both Catholic and Protestant presentations of human destiny. Some, however, have held that in the long run all of us will be so purified as to be able to enjoy everlasting union with God, which is the essence of the Christian hope. Among the ancients, Origen, the most original, creative, and gifted theologian in the early Church, believed that not only we humans but even Satan and all the legions of evil powers in the universe should eventually so qualify. In more recent times various bodies of Christians, such as the Universalists, have taught that all men and women are to be reconciled to God at the last and enjoy his nearer presence. If then our destiny is so favorably assured in the long run, why worry about salvation, whatever it may mean?

Another view of human destiny, which finds clear support in the writings of Paul and has been held by various individual Christians and some Christian groups, is that those who do not "make the grade" are simply extinguished; they simply die. Many people, though they may think they enjoy life heartily, do not wish for any resurrection or immortality, so the prospect of such annihilation, far from holding any terrors for them, may seem quite welcome. Such people naturally ask, "What is there to be saved from?"

Even before we are ready to consider in any detail the Christian doctrine of "Last Things," we can already see that the notion of salvation presupposes that humankind is in an unsatisfactory state. The word *salvation* is etymologically connected with the Latin word *salus*, which means simply health, welfare, a general state of well-being. The idea of salvation as presented in the Bible and the Creed would be nonsensical apart from the underlying presupposition that humankind is notably not as it should be. Classically, the moral disease of humankind that inclines us to do the wrong when we know it is against our own best interest, let alone the good of society, is expressed in the now misleading phrase "original sin."

The biblical way of accounting for our being in such a state is to be found, of course, in the story of the Fall of Adam and Eve, prototypes of the human race. Educated Christians have usually taken the story in an allegorical sense and surely what we now know about the evolution of man confirms such an allegorical interpretation. Few today could suppose, if anyone ever really did, that there was a "first man" who underwent a surgical operation at the hands of God, resulting in the manufacture of Eve, the "first woman," or that at the bidding of a serpent she tempted her mate with a slice of fruit from a tree, resulting in the moral degradation not only of them but of all their progeny, that is, of the entire human race. Of course the story is allegorical, but the truth for which the allegory stands is so indisputable that G. K. Chesterton once called the doctrine of original sin the only Christian doctrine that is empirically verifiable.

The human race, for all its extraordinary potentialities and for all its marvellous achievements in science and civilization, in art and literature, in music and architecture, has such an astounding capacity for self-destruction that thousands of years ago, long before modern technology was conceivable and long before modern ecology has shown how recklessly humankind destroys whatever environment it gets, thinking people perceived in one way or another that there is something rotten in the human makeup. To make that sort of suggestion is not and never was mere self-deprecation. On the contrary, it is only because we have obviously such stupendous capacities for good, such marvellous powers of reason, and such creative abilities as are peerless in all the known universe around us, that the question of our inbuilt corruption ever arises. We know we are not as we ought to be. Otherwise our planet would be much more of a paradise than it is; certainly there would be no wars.

Some have put their total trust in education, believing that people are so naturally good that ignorance is all that stands in the way of their achieving a perfect society. Six hundred years before the birth of Christ, Confucius, one of the greatest human sages of all time so believed and from him indeed stemmed the immensely impressive system of Chinese education that came to be the wonder of the world. He was given an opportunity to put his theories into practice, for he was accorded an administrative position somewhat like that of a State governorship. He promptly abolished the army and the police force and provided more and more education. The result was disastrous. In his old age he was nevertheless given a second opportunity, with almost exactly the same results. What the great Confucius did not adequately appreciate is that humanity's plight is due not so much to mere lack of knowledge as to a basic corruption of the human will.

Paul saw the root of the trouble: "I cannot understand my own behavior," he writes. "I fail to carry out the things I want to do, and I find myself doing the very things I hate" (Rom. 7:15, JB). Paul recognizes that we humans are not masters of our own situation. He sees within him a lower and a higher self, the one at war with the other. Pascal, a seventeenth-century genius, saw a human being as a monster with one foot in the dunghill and the other leaping up to heaven, a monster who is half brute, half angel. One does not expect a dog to write poetry or a cat to design churches; animals behave according to a pattern that is, generally speaking, predictable. In them is not the absurd tension between grandiose aims and vicious practices. They have not "eaten of the fruit of the tree of good and evil." Human beings, by contrast, are living paradoxes. As a more modern writer has put it:

> *Within my earthly temple there's a crowd:*
> *There's one of us who's humble, one who's proud;*
> *There's one who's broken-hearted for his sins,*
> *And one who, unrepentant, sits and grins;*
> *There's one who loves his neighbor as himself,*
> *And one who cares for naught but fame and pelf.*
> *From much corroding care I should be free,*
> *If once I could determine which is me.*

Moreover, I am caught in a bind of my own making. I am like a spider trapped in its own web. There is, in Sartre's memorable phrase, "no exit." People in the ancient world were no less conscious of all this than are thinking people today. They saw that the world, for all "the glory that was Greece and the grandeur that was Rome," was old and tired and in a sorry mess. Every nostrum had been tried. The plight of humanity was not for lack of sages or builders or seekers after truth. There were many of all of these. The human plight remained. It still remains. One need not be a cranky prophet of doom to fear for the future of humankind today. From both a scientific and a commonsense standpoint the prospect is precarious. Few well-informed people would care to bet much on human survival through the twenty-first century. What is promised to Christians is not that the basic human problem will go away, but that, because a way has been found *for those who believe in Christ and follow him,* personal hope is justified. This does not mean that there is nothing left for me to do. On the contrary, I must indeed work out my salvation "with fear and trembling" (Phil. 2:12, KJV). The difference is that I am assured that my "labour is not in vain in the Lord" (I Cor. 15:58, KJV).

The world will indeed come to an end, sooner or later, but Christ, who has promised to be with his Church "even unto the end of the world" (Matt. 28:20, KJV), has snatched us out of the world so that we may have the capacity, through him, to survive the world's end.

Such is the meaning of salvation to the Christian. Whatever the fate in store for humanity at large, Christ has made the impossible possible for us. The ancients understood human alienation from God as the result of the Fall of humanity in the Garden of Eden. Today our insight is enlarged by evolutionary and existentialist thought. Suffice it to say that we are stuck on the way to our goal and that through Christ God has made possible our redemption. With awesome divine humility God emptied himself, divested himself in such a way as "to fit his stature to our need" by entering our human condition and so removing the barrier that lay in the way of our advance. Jews and Muslims agree that God has spoken through his prophets, revealing through their words something of his nature and purposes for humankind. But for Christians the supreme mode of his unfolding is his entry into humanity as one of us, bridging the gulf between God and humankind and providing us with hope that would otherwise be the merest whistling in the dark. To hear through God's prophets that he cares for us is one thing. It is a consoling notion. But to have God take definitive action by condescending to be born into our human race and "to pitch his tent among us" in such a way as to unfold to us his divine nature is something very different and, to Christian faith, overwhelming.

The difference is infinite. We catch only a mere glimpse of it in the difference we can all readily see between (1) my shouting from a safe distance the directions to the fire escape while you scream for help in a burning building and (2) my leaping into the building, sharing your misery and your terror while lifting you bodily out to safety. The history of Christian thought repeatedly discloses the personal awakening of the greatest Christian saints to the meaning of rescue from the human predicament. Augustine felt he had been so rescued *inter pontem et fontem* (between the bridge and the river), and John Wesley believed himself to have been "snatched like a brand from the burning."

Salvation, then, however it be understood, is always salvation from a terrible plight. The process by which God accomplished his saving purpose for humankind was long and arduous. The "coming down from heaven" was only the beginning of it. It entailed, as we shall see, the most profound anguish and the sharpest pain a human being can suffer, and eventually complete fulfilment of the divine purpose and total victory for God's plan for "our salvation." It is a gift available to humankind at large; yet by no means all necessarily appropriate it.

> *SAVE me, God! The water*
> *is already up to my neck!*
> *I am sinking in the deepest swamp,*
> *there is no foothold;*
> *I have stepped into deep water*
> *and the waves are washing over me.*
>   —Psalm 69:1–2 (JB)

> *LORD! Save me!*
>   —Peter to Jesus,
>   Matthew 14:30 (JB)

CHAPTER VII

The Virgin Birth

*And was incarnate by the Holy Ghost of the Virgin Mary,
and was made man*

THE doctrine of the Virgin Birth (that is, the assertion that Mary, the mother of Jesus, conceived him in her womb without any human male cooperation) seems to those who account themselves "liberal" in their approach to Christian faith a peculiarly incredible, not to say ludicrous notion and perhaps the most conspicuous obstacle to an acceptance of the traditional Catholic view. Embarrassment about this doctrine, however, is not entirely confined to "liberals"; many thoughtful "conservatives," Roman Catholic and Reformed, Anglican and Lutheran, feel ill at ease with it. It seems at first sight so obviously alien to everything that we know in biology. How important is this doctrine for anyone who feels committed to an orthodox, traditionalist understanding of the Christian faith?

First, let us look at what has been generally affirmed by those who insist on taking the virgin birth of Christ as an historical event. Belief in it as an historical event is doubtless ancient and has been traditionally taken to be well grounded in Scripture. The Fathers of the Church all accepted it as a matter of course. In the early centuries of the Church only a few heretical sects, such as the Adoptianists and the Psilanthropists, denied it, and it is noteworthy that all these sects, in one way or another, also denied the central doctrine of the divinity of Christ. Broadly speaking, indeed, one might say that the strength of insistence on the Virgin

Birth has been commensurate with emphasis on the uniqueness of Christ as "the only-begotten Son of God." Theological arguments adduced in support of belief in the Virgin Birth of Christ have generally rested on two basic contentions: (1) the doctrine is a fitting pointer to, not to say the indispensable accompaniment of, what is affirmed in the central doctrine of the Incarnation, and (2) since all things are possible with God, there is no reason why he should not use his power to provide whatever would be the special circumstance suited to the most crucial event in human history: the entry of God into humanity. Some have even suggested that it would seem more odd and more astonishing for God to have neglected so to mark the uniqueness of his coming to earth than for him to have so marked it. In short, such contentions usually imply that the reason people find difficulty with the Virgin Birth is that they do not really accept the Incarnation, apart from which it would be pointless. Moreover, for many the fact that Scripture seems to teach the doctrine of the Virgin Birth plainly makes any argument unnecessary.

In considering the case for such an interpretation of the traditional doctrine, we must not overlook certain historical circumstances. For instance, in the religious ambience in which the doctrine was developed, virginity was held in high esteem. To the ancients the claim to virgin birth seemed apposite to the emergence of one who claimed divinity. Virgin birth sat well with such a claim.

More importantly, however, the ancients held a view about human reproduction that is radically incompatible with all we know today about that biological process: they took the female partner to be *almost* a passive receptacle[1] and the male to be the sole active element, the sole agent in the reproductive process. So Jesus could be said to be incarnate by the Holy Spirit as the sole agent of his conception in the womb of Mary, its virgin receptacle. The consequences for theology of that biological error have been striking. That the ancients were so mistaken on this point does not in itself absolutely exclude the possibility of their being right in their

---

1. Aristotle does seem to recognize (*De Generatione*, 730a) that the female contributes some "material," but the influence of so weak and casual a suggestion against so strong and widespread a prejudice would be minimal even among those who knew that work.

adherence to the doctrine of the Virgin Birth, and we shall see presently that there are new considerations that could be proposed in favor of it; but it does warrant our being more than ordinarily wary of their theological opinions on all questions relating to the conception and birth of Jesus.

The "female receptacle" view spawned a variety of subquestions. Would not the receptacle itself require a purity fitting for the special action of God? Would it be enough for Mary to be technically a virgin, in the sense of having "known no man," that is, of never having engaged in sexual intercourse? No: she must also, many felt, remain for ever virginal, so excluding the possibility of uterine brothers or sisters for Jesus. This doctrine that Mary is "ever-virgin" is a development also dependent on the "female receptacle" view. If the womb is simply a place for the reception of the fertilizing agent (normally for the male sperm but in this unique case for the action of the Holy Spirit of God himself), its purity has a significance and importance far beyond what can be readily grasped by us in the light of our modern biological knowledge. To get into the mind of the ancients on this point, we must first try to think ourselves into their mistaken biological stance.

Logic based upon these ancient biological views led some to go on to speculate that even perpetual virginity was not enough for the unique receptacle that Mary was. She must have been in some miraculous way prepared by a "precleansing" even before her own birth in the womb of her mother, Anna. This precleansing could have been accomplished by her exemption from the "stain" of original sin that is otherwise universal in the human race. That Mary was so exempted at *her* conception in *her* mother's womb is what is expressed in the doctrine of the Immaculate Conception.

By no means all medieval theologians subscribed to this doctrine. Among those who opposed it was the most celebrated of all, Thomas Aquinas, and his fellow Dominicans naturally followed him on this point. Opposition to the doctrine of the Immaculate Conception was, however, technical, receiving much of its support from appeal to Scripture: Paul, for instance, affirms that all humanity has sinned (Rom. 3:23; 5:12, 18; II Cor. 5:14). Augustine and the Fathers generally held that this included every human being. Nevertheless, they exempted Jesus who, though fully human, was "without sin."

The proponents of the doctrine of the Immaculate Conception had nevertheless formidable weight on their side, so long as
the "female receptacle" notion prevailed, as it did up to comparatively recent times. They could argue, for instance, that when
Augustine and Paschasius Radbertus specifically affirmed that
Mary's flesh was "flesh of sin," and when Fulgentius asserted that
she was "conceived in sin according to the usual law of human
nature," they were not carrying through the logical consequences
of the doctrine of the Virgin Birth as seen from the standpoint of
the "female receptacle" view of human biology.

The question of the Immaculate Conception of Mary remained controversial not only throughout the Middle Ages but till
the nineteenth century. The great Council of Trent, held in
1549–60 in reaction to the earlier phase of the Reformation movement, refrained from officially promulgating it as Roman Catholic
Church doctrine. Nevertheless, in 1854, Pius IX, notorious to later
historians for his prelatical authoritarianism and theological ignorance, simply proclaimed *ex motu proprio*, without support from
any general council of the Roman Catholic Church and against the
opinion of many of the most learned theologians of the day within
that church, that assent to the doctrine of the Immaculate Conception was henceforth to be *required* of every Roman Catholic. Pius
IX, in taking that step, was preparing the way for an even more
startling one, which he took at the First Vatican Council (1869–
70), by asserting that the Pope is personally infallible when he
makes pronouncements about faith and morals in the name of the
Church (*ex cathedra*), and that he needs neither guidance from
theologians nor advice from councils in reaching whatever decision
on these matters he may choose to reach. More than a hundred
bishops left Rome prematurely rather than vote against the Pope's
wishes on this matter, as many of them would have felt in con-
science bound to do.[2]

In the early Church the doctrine of the Virgin Birth emphasized the reverence in which the mother of Jesus was held. The

2.   In the decade before the Second Vatican Council, in my book *The
Vatican Revolution* (Boston: Beacon Press, 1957; London: Macmillan &
Co., Ltd., 1958), I discussed the background and the effects of the notoriously infelicitous action of Pius IX at the First Vatican Council. Both
editions of the book contain, in Appendix II, a discussion in technical
detail of the doctrine of the Immaculate Conception.

Greek Church hailed her as Theotokos, the God-bearer, for she had borne the Child who was God himself. No one who believed in the divinity of Christ could deny Mary this beautiful title. The Latins, overlooking the subtlety of the Greek designation ("the Bearer of God"), translated it *Mater Dei*, "Mother of God." The linguistic confusion gave rise to excesses in popular devotion. Mary, according to official teaching, could properly be called "the one who bore God," but she could not properly be called "God's mother," since "mother" means *also* "female parent" and implies a line of succession. It also indirectly implies a male parent which Jesus, according to official teaching, did not have. The "female receptacle" theory, however, made people generally less troubled by such reflections than we must be today. The consequences of the confusion may be seen in a popular devotion that emerged honoring Anna, Mary's mother, as "the Grandmother of God"!

Now let us turn to modern biology. Apart from all theological questions, is the concept of parthenogenesis or virgin birth in humans intelligible according to what we know today? In lower forms of life, asexual reproduction occurs. In higher forms of life, simple stimulation, naturally or artificially, of the ovum can cause it to divide and reproduce. The nucleus of the ovum pairs with the nucleus of the second polar body, after the second division, to form a complete set of chromosomes. The simple fusion of two cleavage cells or the duplication of the chromosomes at another stage can also cause reproduction. Thus, parthenogenesis is no longer a merely theoretical concept. It has been performed with many different plants and animals, including rabbits. It has not so far been practiced with humans; but a few scientists think that this sort of reproduction is not absolutely unimaginable, even that it might occur spontaneously, in rare instances, in humans. We must note that the parthenogenetic offspring of a woman, even if it could occur, would be, in all probability, female. Nevertheless, it may not be *totally* impossible that it should be male, in an extraordinary case. It might be male if, for example, the ovum had already reached a stage of overmaturity, or if one of the X chromosomes had been somehow eliminated in the process of division.[3]

3. For these observations on the possibility of human parthenogenesis I am indebted to my friend Daniel Claes, M.D. (Harvard).

Although these may seem speculative ideas, we should not forget that many now established scientific procedures were for long accounted speculative. The notion of "test tube" babies, for instance, was widely so regarded till a baby was born to an Englishwoman, Lesley Brown, on July 25, 1978: the first authenticated "test tube" baby in history.

Since we have been looking at the possibility of human parthenogenesis and the biological problems connected with it, let us glance also at another notion that would have been unthinkable to the ancients but is now much before the minds of biologists: cloning. Cloning has already been accomplished in frogs. Its extension to humans, though probably by no means imminent, is certainly not entirely inconceivable. Cloning is achieved by the removal of the nucleus of an ovum and the substitution of either (1) any other cell from any other tissue of the female's body, or (2) a cell from the body of another of the same species, for example, a male. In the former case the clone would always be female, because the enucleated ovum would contain no chromosomes and the other cell from the female's own body would contain only female (XX) chromosomes. To produce a male clone one would need the male cell with the enucleated ovum, as in (2), so as to provide the necessary male (XY) chromosomes. Not even by human cloning, therefore, if it could be accomplished, could a male child be produced without the aid of a man, and if such aid were used the child would be a clone of the male donor, not of the female.

A human virgin birth, however unlikely, is not so utterly absurd a notion from a strictly scientific point of view as almost every biologist a century ago would have insisted. Odd as it may seem to many, the major difficulties with the traditional understanding of the Christian doctrine of the Virgin Birth are not scientific but theological. We must now, therefore, consider them.

First, we should notice that, even if one case of human parthenogenesis were scientifically authenticated today (especially if it were a male child), it would damage the traditional understanding of the doctrine of the Virgin Birth, not support it. If such parthenogeneses in humans became relatively common, they would injure the Church's tradition even more. For the whole point of the doctrine lies in its betokening the uniqueness of the birth of Jesus Christ. One other human virgin birth would destroy that uniqueness. This, by the way, is a point that Antony Flew and other contemporary analytical philosophers have failed to perceive in their discussions of the question. To make sense of the traditional understanding of the Virgin Birth of Christ, what we should need would be scientific evidence that such a birth could occur in some way that would be scientifically intelligible, not that it has ever occurred or that its occurrence is in the least likely.

An even weightier theological objection is that, even if an asexual, parthenogenic birth could occur, the offspring, though it might pass for human for all ordinary purposes, would not meet the technical requirements of classic Christian theology that Jesus is both fully divine and fully human. What is meant by "fully human" ("True Man" as the old theological language has it) is a separate difficulty, of course, since we are less certain today, in the light of evolutionary biology, what would constitute "perfect humanity" than were the ancients. Still, presumably few would dispute that a eunuch or a mental defective would fall short of any standard of what it means to be "fully human." But what of, say, a human clone, if one were possible? Modern theologian Karl Rahner has given some attention to questions of this sort, and ethicist Paul Ramsey has discussed some of the moral implications of "fabricated man." At least we must take very seriously the question whether a child born apart from the normal process of procreation, involving the coming together of sperm and ovum, would be "fully human."

Here we must not overlook the fact that the ancients and medieval people could not have properly understood the point in question. They knew nothing of either ovum or sperm cells. Not till 1797 did William Cumberland Cruikshank discover the ovum in mammals. Moreover, despite official Church insistence on the perfect humanity of Jesus, the tendency of the ancients and of the men of the Middle Ages to forget the humanity in practice and emphasize the divinity is not surprising in view of their tendency to look on the female role as almost that of an incubator. So, if God himself were accounted the sole agent in the miraculous process of the Incarnation, whatever it was, then of course Jesus would be considered predominantly divine, to say the least.

Historically, this is precisely what occurred in popular practice, whatever the learned might say in their working hours. We know, for instance, from the history of Christian theology, and we can see from the history of Christian art, that the doctrine of the Virgin Birth, accompanied by the faulty scientific views of the ancient world, gave rise to a general tendency to move away from official orthodoxy ("True God and True Man") into an exaltation of the divinity of Christ. This tendency is dramatically observable in, for example, the departure from the "Good Shepherd" iconography of ancient and early medieval Christian art and the development instead of the Divine Judge imagery of Michelangelo's painting. With this development in theology and the arts went another. Mary was more and more assigned the role of mediatrix between the people and her divine Son. Only in recent times has the Roman Catholic Church sought to correct that tendency, which sprang from the *way* in which the Virgin Birth had been interpreted.

Many modern theologians have questioned the traditional understanding of the doctrine of the Virgin Birth on the ground that it does injury to the full humanity of our Lord. Even Karl Barth, a doughty champion of the traditionalist view of this subject, insists that it is nevertheless impossible for us to say that the Incarnation had by absolute necessity to take the form of this miraculous occurrence. Barth's concern is above all to insist that nothing must be said to obscure or weaken in any way the theological truth that the nature that God assumed in Christ is identical with our nature.

We must now look at the scriptural evidence in light of modern biblical scholarship. No reference to the Virgin Birth occurs in any of the epistles. Moreover, no reference to it occurs in either Mark or John. Such evidence from Scripture as we have comes from the nativity narratives of Matthew and Luke, and even those of us who are most open to the miraculous can see good reason to question the notion that the Matthaean and Lucan birth narratives are to be taken as entirely historical, since the evangelists' intention to be understood allegorically is at certain points so obvious. When we compare what the first apostles of the Christian Way had to say about the Resurrection, acceptance of which was virtually identified with acceptance of the apostolic proclamation, with their total silence on this other subject, it is difficult to believe that they could have accounted it crucially important. It is easy, indeed, to conclude that either they did not think it very important at all or else never even mentioned it in the course of their preaching at any time.

Furthermore, modern biblical scholars also have good reason to question the use of the word *virgin*, with all its specific connotations, as an acceptable translation of the original, which does not by any means necessarily carry these connotations but can simply mean "young woman" or "maiden," a term habitually used in respect of any unmarried woman. Neither the Hebrew word *betullah* nor the Greek word *parthenos* specifies, in normal usage, what we mean by virginity. They would be more accurately rendered "girl," and indeed modern versions and translations tend in this direction: the Revised Standard Version, for instance, has "young woman" with a footnote "or virgin," while the Jerusalem Bible has "maiden," in texts such as Isaiah 7:14, traditionally taken by Christian exegetes to be a prophecy of the coming of Christ.

One must also bear in mind that in early Hebrew as in other primitive societies girls were normally married very early, shortly after puberty, so that the question of virginity or nonvirginity did not arise as it does in our minds. Virginity was in any case negatively regarded in that society. In the New Testament, however, it is occasionally lauded as an admirable ideal. This admiration reflects certain ascetic outlooks that had by then emerged even in the generally traditionalist climate of Palestine, apart from which acceptance of teachers and prophets such as John the Baptist would have been impossible. In the climate in which Christianity spread, virginity did have a high religious significance.

To say the least, then, while Christians can appeal with confidence to Scripture on the subject of the Resurrection of Christ, they cannot so usefully invoke it on the question of the Virgin Birth. When all that is said, however, Christians cannot escape the fact that from very early times in Christian history our tradition certainly laid much store by the doctrine of the Virgin Birth as a pivot of orthodoxy. Whether it is to be taken as an historical event (miraculous, of course) or accepted as a symbol of the uniqueness of Christ, the words of the Nicene Creed ("incarnate by the Holy Ghost of the Virgin Mary") say something that in one way or another is of fundamental importance for all who seriously profess the Christian faith. At the very least they say: "This man Jesus, born of Mary, was not merely a man; he was God made flesh. Through the action of the Holy Spirit God *became* man in the Person of Christ." The emphasis has always been on the words "and was made man." It is at these words that good Western tradition has always dictated the most profound gesture of reverence, for here we are at the heart of the mystery of Christian faith, the opening scene in the drama of the life of Christ, the *sine qua non* of all that to which the New Testament writers and the Church Fathers bear witness.

We have seen in earlier chapters and in more than one way how much more amenable to a "spiritual" understanding of all things is modern physics, compared with the physics of either Aristotle or that of the mechanistic scientists of the eighteenth and nineteenth centuries. What we now know from modern physics enables us to avoid looking on "matter" in the old "intractable stuff" way. Many of the old puzzles in philosophical theology have gone; their solution has not come about from more and more careful philosophical analysis or theological subtlety but, rather, from the revolution in physics. What seemed in the old days to be possible only by the direct action of God through his "overruling" the "laws of nature" can now be seen in many instances to be an aspect of the general wonder of all things in a universe far more marvellous than our forefathers could have imagined even in their dreams. We who are open to the notion that God can do anything through a special use of the wonderful processes of nature, without recourse to the absurdities of primitive "folklore magic," must surely be ready to look at whatever possibilities biologists can suggest to us. We have seen how much more hospitable to certain "religious" ideas is modern physics compared to the old mechanistic kind. Modern biology, though perhaps less obviously hospitable in many cases, is not really a serious obstacle in this one. The more troublesome difficulties come from the theological side.

We must take these difficulties seriously and consider without prejudice whether the doctrine of the Virgin Birth might be better understood figuratively, where it makes a great deal of sense and points to a beautiful and important truth. Must the consequences of such a view, with its implications for the biological ancestry of our Lord Jesus Christ, profoundly shock us? If God used a human father as well as the acknowledged and superlatively revered human mother, Mary, in the admittedly miraculous process we call the Incarnation, must we take that as a diminishment of the grounds of our belief in the divinity of Christ? After all, it is the Incarnation itself that is the central difficulty for unbelievers, much as was the crucifixion, as Paul noted, an obstacle to the Jews and madness to the pagans (I Cor. 1:23).

What even if Jesus were an illegitimate child, as vulgar rumor has often naturally enough suggested? Illegitimacy has been widely disparaged for various sociological and other reasons; nevertheless, a number of the greatest men in history have been born out of wedlock. Why should such a notion be so peculiarly offensive in the case of Jesus? On the strictest orthodox view, God entered humanity in the humblest circumstances. He was born of a poor Jewish girl. His birth took place in a stable. Before his ministry he worked at manual labor. Could it injure the Son of God to be also born without benefit of a legal marriage? If, as all Christian piety acknowledges, he stooped to our human state by accepting to be born of a woman, dare we be so arrogant as to suppose it to be beneath his dignity to accept human paternity too? We have seen why the ancients, because of their presuppositions, could not look on the matter in such a way; but why should not we? The important element in the tradition is surely that the coming of Christ had to be inconspicuous: "How silently, how silently, the wondrous gift is given!" Does not the obscurity matter much more than the technical virginity?

Many people today would say yes unhesitatingly. If we do say it, however, we should at least hesitate. Whatever view we take, in face of all that we have considered, let our humble response be in the spirit of the words of Mary: "Behold the handmaid of the Lord: be it unto me according to thy word."

Then must the last word on this thorny topic be no more than a take-it-or-leave-it? If the traditional doctrine under question had been about anything farther away from the Incarnation of God in Christ, from that encampment of God among us that is the focus of our Christian faith, then perhaps we could so leave wide open the result of the inquiry we have been conducting in the present chapter. But since its function has always been and always must be to point to the uniqueness of the Incarnation, we must be more cautious than that. While we may concede with Barth and others that there may be no ground for holding that the birth of Christ had by absolute necessity to be accomplished in so miraculous a way as tradition has represented it, dare we say, after all, that a Christian can lightly write off the traditional understanding of the doctrine? Surely not. At the least we must surely say that this doctrine, however it is to be interpreted, represents something that is so near the heart of our faith that to treat it lightly is to steer us away from all that is vital to our faith, all the foundation apart from which our faith would crumble to ashes.

A final point is worthy of mention. We all know that, though the Hebrews were perhaps less extreme in their attitudes of male dominance than were their neighboring societies, the ancients were all, by modern standards, very much disinclined to give women anything like the freedom they now more and more enjoy in societies such as our own in America and Western Europe. When we reflect on their misunderstanding of the female role in reproduction, what would otherwise seem mere chauvinism becomes more understandable, however regrettable some will account it. It is in the light of this historical circumstance that we must look at the extraordinary exaltation of Mary, specially selected by God as the sole human vehicle for the Incarnation. In their insistence on the Virgin Birth, the ancients were not only exalting womankind, they were pointing to the new life that this event was to bring to humankind. The new life of humanity begins with a startling break from the past. From time immemorial the seed of males had perpetuated the race; now came a break in the series: one solitary instance, but one that was to usher in the new age. The special role traditionally assigned to Mary is not only a pointer to the uniqueness of Christ and a symbol of the exaltation of all women, but a blazing of the trail to the new dispensation. So Mary celebrates her joy as she "magnifies the Lord": "For he hath regarded the lowliness of his handmaiden. For behold, from henceforth all generations shall call me blessed. . . . He hath put down the mighty from their seat, and hath exalted the humble and meek. . . . He remembering his mercy hath holpen his servant Israel; as he promised to our forefathers, Abraham and his seed for ever" (*Book of Common Prayer*).

GRANT, O Lord, we beseech thee, an inviolable firmness of faith to thy people; that as they confess thine only-begotten Son, the everlasting partaker of thy glory, to have been born in our very flesh of the Virgin Mother, they may be delivered from present adversities and admitted into abiding joys; through the same Jesus Christ our Lord.

—Leonine Sacramentary (seventh century)

————CHAPTER VIII————

Self-Emptying Love

And was crucified also for us under Pontius Pilate.
He suffered and was buried

NOT only was Jesus born in humility, his entire live was a humiliation, culminating in the crucifixion, which was not only one of the most cruel forms of torture ever devised by man but also the most ignominious of punishments. When we speak of the suffering of Christ (called in antique language his "Passion"), we usually refer more specifically to the pains he endured immediately leading up to his death on the Cross. His entire life, however, was a humiliation. According to a well-known passage in the letter to the Philippians (Phil. 2:6–8, JB):

> *His state was divine,*
> *yet he did not cling*
> *to his equality with God*
> *but emptied himself*
> *to assume the condition of a slave,*
> *and became as men are;*
> *and being as all men are,*
> *he was humbler yet,*
> *even to accepting death,*
> *death on a cross.*

This is the basic text so much quoted by those theologians who in the nineteenth century expounded a "self-emptying" theory of the Incarnation. The theory they propounded was called "kenotic" from the Greek word *ekenōse* ("emptied") used in the above passage. For various technical reasons the theory, which had been especially popular in certain Anglican and Lutheran circles, lost favor not only among those who, like some of the authors of *The Myth of God Incarnate*, were disinclined to take the doctrine of the Incarnation seriously, but by others of a much more conservative bent.

As I have proposed elsewhere,[1] the kenotic theories on the Incarnation were unsatisfactory, not through their making too much of the self-emptyingness of God, but, rather, through their making too little of it by confining it to this special case. The image they held up before us tended to convey the notion that while God acted in a special and surprising way by humbling himself, emptying himself of his power and other attributes in becoming man "for us men and for our salvation," he did so in an exceptional move. One almost got the impression that, although this move showed how much God cared for his creatures, his act was more a demonstration of his "infinite power" than an expression of his fundamental nature.

As a great king who normally sits on his throne expecting his subjects to wait upon him and prostrate themselves in his august presence may graciously descend to greet a poor cripple who cannot make the proper obeisances, so God, his divine majesty notwithstanding, made the gracious gesture to fallen humankind. Although one would not say the special act was "out of character," one would not expect a king to behave like that habitually and much less would one expect it of God before whose divine majesty the angels veil their faces. The abdication of power was accounted such a special act, gracious though of course it was, that it could not but seem a manifestation of power. To say the least, the kenotic christologies carried echoes of the old model of the divine potentate whose power is so great that he could order the beheading of all the inhabitants of one of his realms (with justice too) by one terrible genocidal decree, but who, like the Governor of a State in commuting a death sentence, magnanimously decided to forgive all subjects not too stubborn or impenitent to accept forgiveness.

The proponents of the kenotic christologies were motivated

---

1. *He Who Lets Us Be: A Theology of Love* (New York: Seabury Press, 1975), pp. 59ff.

partly by their desire to deal with certain questions arising out of the old models. For example, if Jesus was indeed divine as well as human, as traditional orthodoxy insisted, are we not then compelled to say that as a little baby on his mother's knee he was in possession of all the attributes of deity, including omniscience? Did he only *look* helpless and ignorant as does every baby, when in fact he knew everything and could do anything? Did he have nothing to learn, as do the rest of us, being as infinitely wise when he was a week old as when he was thirty? A typical answer of the kenoticists was that God emptied himself of these attributes in Jesus and then gradually assumed them again as he "grew, and waxed strong in spirit, filled with wisdom," (Luke 2:40, KJV). An inevitable and formidable objection to such proposals is that they dilute the significance of the classic insistence that Christ is both fully divine and fully human, a doctrine that these theories were intended to reinforce. Unless both the humanity and the divinity of Jesus are taken seriously, God did not truly suffer in and with humankind. Jesus becomes simply one of the many victims of the cruelty and injustice with which humankind treats its greatest teachers and prophets, while God reigns on as a compassionate but aloof Father and Judge.

If, however, we see the self-emptying of God as fundamentally characteristic of his nature, manifested in all his acts, including that of creation, we get a clearer vision of the meaning of the Incarnation. If God, in creating and sustaining each one of us, enters into our situation and suffers in it, abdicating his power so that we may have the freedom to grow and thereby also risking our failure, as a mother lets her child run free even at his peril and to her inward anguish, then the Incarnation can be seen in another light. It becomes no longer a special case, an exceptional move, but a manifestation "in the flesh" of the eternal activity of God. Never again could one indulge in speculations such as that if humankind had not fallen in the Garden of Eden or otherwise, the Incarnation would have been unnecessary.

This larger view of the self-emptyingness of God also reassures us in our own sufferings, for we no longer see God as entering into human flesh and heroically enduring whatever Jesus had to endure; we can now see him entering into and suffering in, with, and for us *all the time*, and in even the most trivial of our woes. The very nature of God is so transmogrified for us through this greater vision that the mystery of the Incarnation, though revealed to us in the life and death of Jesus Christ, is not a solitary case, not a deviation from a "normal" state of affairs, but an eternal mystery, one that cannot be confined to any temporal duration such as the thirty-three years of human life traditionally assigned to Jesus, but one that is at the very heart of all things, though made known to us in the unique action God took for us in Christ. This truth lies hidden behind the Catholic tradition of the Eucharist or Mass as an ongoing process. Of course the Mass could not have been begun but for the entry of God into humanity in Christ, for only in that way could our doltish and wilful humankind have apprehended the nature of God; nevertheless, time was not when God was not emptying himself and suffering in, with, and for his creatures.

In short, to use a convenient symbol, the Cross is not only a piece of wood on a hill near Jerusalem, but it is an eternal, flaming reality in the heart of God. To see this as more than just an interesting aside in an inspiring sermon but, rather, as the very core of our belief about the nature and character of God takes effort and time. It is not something we can easily grasp, for it revolutionizes the thinking of most of us. Yet apart from it our thought about God and about his coming in Christ to save us is bound to be distorted and primitive in a way unworthy of us to whom he has sent the "true light" of Christ.

As we hear the proclamation that our Lord suffered, we fail to grasp its full significance unless we recognize that he who so suffered was not just another martyr, another victim of human idiocy and human blindness, but the paradigm case: God himself voluntarily choosing to debase himself by sharing our condition in human flesh because that is what, in one way or another, he is always and by his own nature eternally predisposed to do. As an erring young woman (a drug addict, perhaps) learns with surprise that her mother or father has gone half round the world to come to her rescue and then gradually recognizes that this is not just a special, astonishing gesture, but what in fact her parents have been doing all along, so we discover, through the revelation that "God was in Christ," that the self-abnegating act of the Incarnation is by any reckoning "typical of God."

Jesus taught that we must lose our life in order to find it. But this is not just a paradoxical admonition; it is a fundamental moral law of the universe, whose source is the heart of God himself. It works not because doing it pleases God who then rewards us for our obedience to his command; it works because, when we follow the precept, we are following a fundamental principle of Being. For God, who is the source of all other beings, is habitually engaged in such self-renunciation. Only at the lower levels of being do we find the constant assertion of rights and the habitual insistence on self-preservation. At the higher levels we find, rather, a willingness to yield, a preparedness to set aside one's rights, even a readiness to lay down one's life for one's friends. A father who gives a kidney to save a daughter's life is neither simply obeying a text in the Bible nor doing something he cannot help because of his love for his child; he is working with God in the way that things are, deep in the very heart of God.

It is a sort of moral streamlining. The early designs of the automobile were, by modern standards, clumsy and a little ridiculous. That was because the designers were trying to follow the pattern of the old horse-and-buggy, adapting it to the "horseless carriage." The more streamlined versions that were later developed were more efficient because they obeyed nature; they worked with nature instead of against it. The mature person learns to work with God, not merely to do what God commands.

The nature of God is symbolized in the ancient Catholic devotion to the Sacred Heart. This devotion, despite the infelicitous iconography with which it is much associated today, is extremely profound, for it recognizes that the heart of God beats forever for all beings and is eternally seeking out ways to come to their aid. It is because God is perpetually suffering with his creatures that worldly priests and other clergy who live cozy, unmistakably materialistic lives while preaching on the Cross of Christ without a flicker of the light of Christ illumining them at any point and without a vestige of malaise as they proceed (not to say *process*) from the altar to the luncheon whose sumptuousness troubles them only because of the weight they may gain, look so blasphemous and contemptible to those attuned to the ways of God, who will turn himself inside out for the lowliest of his creatures.

The most terrible experience we humans must all face is that of dying, of giving up life itself and accepting death. God in Christ, the Creed reminds us, did not shrink from sharing even that final affront. Birth and death are the two most un-Godlike experiences known to us, for they accost us with the absurdity of our human situation. They bring out before us the ludicrous limitation of human life, taunting us as they do with our helplessness. Death comes to all: king and beggar, learned and simple, rich and poor, foolish and wise. Much of our life is spent pretending death is not there or (if we cannot go so far) at least that it is not important, being a mere walking off the stage, when in fact we know it is so fearful an ending to all our hopes and ambitions, good and bad alike, that we simply do not dare face its meaning. The Creed reminds us that Jesus Christ not only suffered but died and was buried. God, the source of all life, consented to undergo even this last supremely absurd indignity: to yield up life, to suffer death and finally to be laid out, dressed in a shroud and placed in a tomb. This too is part of the divine drama of the self-emptying of God.

According to a picturesque tradition not represented in the Nicene Creed (though it occurs in the so-called Apostles' Creed), Christ, on his death, descended to the abode of the dead (what the Hebrews called *Sheol* and the Greeks *Hades*) and preached to "the spirits in prison" (cf. I Pet. 3:19; 4:6, JB). In the fourth century, Cyril of Jerusalem interpreted this to mean that Christ went thither to draw the waiting souls of the righteous up with him, releasing them from their chains. We may even go so far, if we are so disposed, as to see in this "Harrowing of Hell" (as it came to be called in medieval language) a self-emptying that went beyond even the experience of dying and the event of death itself to the experience of complete God-forsakenness, of which Christ had a foretaste on the Cross when he cried out, "My God, my God, why hast thou forsaken me?" God himself voluntarily accepts the most terrible of all conditions a creature can know, that of being cut off from the source of all Good. Whether or not we may think this tradition fanciful, at least it brings out for us most strikingly what it means to be the self-emptying God, who stoops to conquer even in creating us and never ceases to do so thereafter, come what may, participating in even the lowest depths of our degradation, lower than the most abject misery, lower than even the valley of death: the utter darkness of being cut off from the source of all Good, the stark horror of leaving the magnetic field of God's love and hurtling in disarray into the eternal gloom of separation that is hell.

Let us look at all this in other terms. God, in whom there is no vestige of selfishness or egocentricity but only the eternal out-pouring of selfless love, so humbly enters into the self-centeredness of his creatures as to know the sharp sadness their self-centeredness brings. God, who is infinitely self-humbling, consents for our sake to know what it means to eat the bitter fruits of pride. God, "the author of peace and lover of concord," volun-tarily puts himself in the maelstrom of war and strife. Therefore, when in any human being we see even the slightest hint of such self-abnegation, we can know we are in the presence of God's action in one of his saints. We can know also that, if we have even the power to perceive this, we are ourselves coming close to God, for only those upon whom God's self-humbling is closing in have eyes to see such glory.

The "hard sayings" of the gospel, such as "turning the other cheek," are icy hard because we understand them so negatively. When we read that we are to turn the other cheek, we read it as though we were being told *not* to fight back. Only those who stand close to the windows of God whence pour forth the radiance of his humility know how much more positive is the injunction, which means, rather, that true love fights with such love and patience that it can endure any blows in the interest of achieving victory for that love, which is incessantly self-humbling. Self-humbling, far from being merely masochistic, is the most aggressive force in the universe. God's saints are anything other than doormats. What sort of doormat is it that could be called "full of light"?

The crucifix symbolizes more than the cruelty of humankind to its greatest prophets. The Eastern Church emphasizes the crucifix less and the Resurrection more. The Latin Church, whose traditions we in the West predominantly inherit, emphasizes the crucifix. The reason is significant. In the West has been developed a strong awareness of the difference between, on the one hand, man as a political animal and an ethical consciousness, and, on the other, man as a seeker after and worshipper of God. Out of the recognition of this difference was developed slowly but in the long run ineradicably the distinction between Church and State, which, with roots in Augustine's treatise *The City of God*, has come into special prominence in American society. The fury of political controversy, the ruthlessness of political activism, and the deceitful venom of political intrigue have plagued every society and are abundantly present in our own. What the crucifix symbolizes is not only that all humanity seeks to kill God in the very act of flying its political banners, the symbols of the variety of its power mania, but also that the Church of God must ceaselessly proclaim that no political triumphs of this world ever constitute the last word. For beyond them all is the kingdom of God, in the light of which every political victory and every political aim in this topsy-turvy world stands out in shabbiness and deceit. The ancient Carthusian Order symbolizes this in its starkly uncompromising motto: *stat crux, dum volvitur orbis* ("while the world is turned round, the Cross stands"). This does not mean that the Church has nothing to say about injustice; it does mean that what it has to say is far too profound for any political platform and far too shocking for any political ticket on earth. The self-humbling of God is too poignantly relevant to human need for any political party to handle, except by way of abusing it for a political end.

The Nicene Creed emphasizes the burial of Jesus Christ. It was not only that he died, that his death was a reality, but that he was buried. We bury a corpse to put it out of sight, where it can gradually decompose unnoticed without offending our nostrils or our eyes. To bury is to hide away. We humans do not only try to kill God; we want very much to bury him, that is, to put him away out of sight. The power maniacs of the world could never be content with killing their opponents. They must bury them out of sight, so that they may be quickly forgotten. In the burial of Jesus is symbolized this preoccupation of humanity for tucking out of sight all that troubles us by its shining splendor, all that is bright enough to show up our own blemishes and our own greed, our contemptibly petty jealousies and our cheap little lusts, our ego-tripping and our narrowminded selfishness. If we can banish such brightness to a distant land, then that is obviously a step in the direction we want; but best of all the "final solution": burial. The burial of Jesus Christ was the indispensable final outcome, the inescapable end to which all the suffering had always pointed.

Graves and tombs and sepulchres are always cold places in our imagination. Not only are they likely to be physically cold, they are by their very nature places where human love cannot go. Love, no less than envy and hate, must avoid them. Love may linger near the grave; but it knows it cannot go into the grave, where it could find only torment: the anguish of mockery aggravating the pain of bereavement. Such is the self-humbling of God, celebrated in the ancient Creed, that it sends the divine love into the very tomb. He suffered and was buried. God not only submitted even to that; he sought it. Nor is there any time in which he is not seeking self-emptying in one way or another, since such is his very essence.

The meaning of the self-emptying principle is exhibited in its application to Christian ethics. What distinguishes a genuinely Christian ethic from, say, a Marxist or a Nietzschean or a Muslim one, is not that it is more or less "severe" and certainly not that it is more or less concerned with social justice. All societies and the ethical systems to which they claim to subscribe are capable of appalling injustices in practice. The more they wax morally indignant about this or that fashionable social question, the more they seem to be brushing under the carpet some other, often more flagrant, social wrong. Of no society is this more lamentably true than it is of the Christian Church, whose record of dealing out the grossest inequities with one hand while working for moral improvement with the other is notorious. Churchgoers habitually shock uncommitted onlookers and others with what seems their extraordinary aptitude for ferreting out things amiss in Svalbard or Sri Lanka while remaining unconcerned about monstrous injustices at the very heart of their own institutional structure. No wickedness looks worse than ecclesiastical wickedness, for nowhere else could be so conspicuous a disparity as that between the power mania of the unworthy and the self-emptyingness that is the life of the Church. Nowhere else does the apparel of cheap social activism look more chintzy, for nowhere else can it be worn alongside the luminous splendor of the self-emptyingness of the love of God that is at work in the Body of Christ.

All schools of Christian ethics, rigorist or laxist, situationist or contextualist, pale before the burning flame and brilliant light of self-emptying love, the positive force that makes all envies and jealousies so ludicrously petty. Such love also, as Paul says (I Cor. 13:6, JB) "delights in the truth." That is why churchpeople so tragically betray the Household of Faith when they allow it to look like the Temple of Non-Think. The self-emptying love of God, apart from which the Christian Church is but fraud and hoax, makes all that comes near it look tawdry and meretricious, not least the political maneuverings of Church assemblies and the slick little clevernesses of preachers who seem to succeed every time in skirting past the Holy Spirit of God.

Once you have seen the spiritual reality of the self-emptyingness of God even so much as trickle through the hearts and minds of men and women, all arguments about justice and morality will seem beside the point, because justice will have already begun to reign within you and mercy to flow from you. The Cross is at the core of Christian faith not only because Jesus died upon one two thousand years ago, but because it is the mainspring of the very Being of God, who because he is everything can afford to become as nothing.

MAY God grant that I may become nothing.

—Simone Weil

──────CHAPTER IX──────

Resurrection

And the third day he rose again
according to the Scriptures

THE Resurrection of Jesus Christ, however interpreted, is traditionally accounted one of the two central foundations of the Christian faith. Indeed, to say this is to understate the case, for such was the disarray of the disciples on Good Friday that virtually nobody could have believed in Jesus any more. The social shame of the Crucifixion was such that whatever Christian faith there had been up to then must have been almost totally extinguished. Certainly the disciples were not disposed to seeing visions such as are reported. Whatever happened at Easter and however it is interpreted, something occurred that changed all that and became the basis of the apostolic preaching. Paul states the situation succinctly and uncompromisingly: "if Christ has not been raised then our preaching is useless and your believing it is useless. . . . And what is more serious, all who have died in Christ have perished. If our hope in Christ has been for this life only, we are the most unfortunate of all people" (I Cor. 15:14–19, JB).

Earlier in the same chapter Paul provides us with one of the earliest literary witnesses to the Resurrection's being central to the apostolic teaching. Biblical scholars recognize that many passages besides these (e.g., in Acts, Romans, Ephesians, and I Timothy) reflect an extremely early emphasis on the Resurrection of Christ as the basis for everything the apostles were proclaiming, a teach-

ing that had been already firmly established a generation before
even the earliest of the Gospels as we now have them was written.
   We should note at the outset the simple fact that nowhere in
the New Testament is the Resurrection of Christ related as an
occurrence that anyone saw happen. What is recounted is the
discovery that the tomb of Jesus was empty, and also the various
appearances of the Risen Christ, first to the disciples and then,
much later, to Paul. In reading the Gospel stories of "raising from
the dead," we should note, moreover, that some of them, at least,
are to be understood as cures. Jesus himself denied that the raising
of the daughter of Jairus was a "resurrection"; she was not dead
(Matt. 9:18–26; Mark 5:21–43; Luke 8:40–56). By contrast, Jesus
was dead. What we are told of the Resurrection of Jesus is different. His physical body was missing from the tomb and was
never seen again; but he appeared to many, apparently in a
glorified form yet in such a way as enabled them to recognize him
and talk with him. The New Testament accounts leave us in no
doubt that, whatever happened, the disciples did not understand
the Resurrection as either a restoration of Jesus to an earthly life
in the form in which he had previously lived his life or as a series
of visions. Indeed, it is plain that they were not at all inclined to
believe the reports of his having risen from the dead. They were
amazed. Some, notably Thomas, were skeptical (John 20:24f.).
They thought at first that they were seeing a ghost; but eventually
they were persuaded by the evidence of their senses that it was not
a ghost but the complete personality of Jesus (as we might say)
that confronted them.
   There is no doubt that the accounts of the Resurrection appearances vary and seem to conflict. On the road to Emmaus the
disciples talk with a stranger and enjoy his learned commentary on
the Scriptures, which he "opens up" to them. So much do they
enjoy his presence and his conversation that, since it is getting
late, they invite him to dinner and to stay overnight with them.
Not till he has sat down to eat, blessed the bread in the traditional
way, and broken it, do they recognize who it is, and then he
vanishes (Luke 24: 13–35). Mary Magdalene, after she talks to the
angels in the tomb, turns round, and sees Jesus standing there. He
inquires why she is weeping, and she still does not recognize him.

She takes him for the gardener. Only when Jesus calls her by name does she recognize who it is and cries out in love: "Rabboni!" Jesus tells her to report their meeting to the disciples (John 20:11–18).

Then the same evening, while the disciples were in a locked room, Jesus stood among them and they were overjoyed. He greeted them in the customary way: Shalom elechem (Peace be with you). Thomas was not among the disciples that evening, and when they told him of what they had seen he refused to believe, saying that he would not unless he saw and felt the holes the nails had made in Jesus' hands and side. Eight days later he had this opportunity, for Jesus appeared again to the disciples, apparently having passed again through the walls and locked doors of the room, and told Thomas to put his finger into the wounds in his hands and his hand into the wound in his side. Thomas then acclaimed him: "My Lord and my God!" (John 20:24–29). According to another account Jesus ate a piece of fish to show the disciples that he was not a ghost such as they had taken him at first to be (Luke 24:36–43).

Some other features in the Resurrection accounts should be noted. The women, when they discover the tomb empty, see the grave clothes lying undisturbed. It is as if the physical body had melted under them. Where the head and feet would have lain, two angels or beings of light were sitting, one at the head, the other at the feet. From the standpoint of what we expect in empirical narratives, the stories seem filled with strange ingredients and also appear to conflict. At times Jesus seems to go unrecognized; at other times he is instantly recognized. He walks through closed doors and solid walls yet eats fish. For the moment let us simply take note of these oddities and seeming conflicts, keeping them in mind for later consideration in the present chapter.

I would contend that unless we affirm that the Resurrection of Christ is a reality in human history, we might as well either reject the Christian faith entirely or else at most relegate it to a place alongside the numerous religious phenomena in the history of humankind. The question remains, however, what kind of reality is it? Can a Christian be content with suggestions, such as that made by Willi Marxsen of the University of Münster, that the reality is a psychological reality, a realization in the minds of the disciples and others that such was their faith in and love for Jesus and their complete dependence on him that they found him alive in their hearts? Would they say, "He is risen!" as we sometimes sing in a hymn, "Still he comes today"? When I say I do not think we can be content with interpretations of that sort, I do not mean that it is not a possible interpretation. It is not only possible, but very natural and plausible (though, even so, not without difficulties) from a purely empirical standpoint.

Ever since Christianity was rehabilitated in the minds of educated people after the worship of nature and of reason in the eighteenth century, controversy has raged between "conservative" and "liberal" scholars on the way in which the Resurrection of Jesus is to be understood. The former have tended to the extreme of insisting on an occurrence in which the physical body of Jesus was somehow revivified and then after some weeks of appearances to the disciples, levitated to "heaven." The latter, veering to the other extreme, have explained away the narratives and apostolic proclamation as but the dramatic expressions of Jesus' followers in their excitement about their deceased Master. It is noteworthy that both these extremes pose serious questions from more than one point of view, not least when one tries to make sense of them in terms of what the record relates. Neither accords entirely with what the New Testament testifies.

We may turn once again to modern physics as we did in our discussion of the various aspects of the Incarnation. In trying to understand what happened in what Christians love to call "the Easter Event," we find ourselves in a better position than the ancients and even Christians of a century or two ago. Our knowledge of human physiology puts us in a better position still, for we cannot share their crude understanding of the human body as so many pints of water and pounds of fat, or of so much "material substance" spread out into torso and limbs and animated by breathing. We know that the body is so intricate that it cannot be compared at all to any inanimate mass. Even such a mass, because of its nuclear structure, is very different from what the ancients supposed it to be. The human body, with more than twelve billion nerve cells in a three-pound brain, with thirty-five miles of glomerular capillaries in the kidneys, each kidney weighing only about half a pound, with lungs that exhale with every breath a hundred times more carbon dioxide than the atmosphere around the body, with eyes that contain staggering complexities, with male and female reproductive systems that carry genetic messages to future generations while often silent to the immediately following one, and with tissues that have stupendous powers of self-healing and recuperation, such a human body is indeed ill-described as a mass of matter having a peculiar shape and containing so many pints of water and pounds of fat. It is, besides much else, an extremely complex arrangement of energy. The ancients, though they perceived that we are "wonderfully made," had no inkling of the complexities that every medical student learns about today. The human body, if it must be described in slick terms, would be better called a stream of energy than a breathing mass. The ancients' ignorance of medicine, by today's standards, is especially notable. And it continued to be so, right down to little more than a century ago.

All that does little to make the notion of the Resurrection of Christ any easier to interpret, but at least it points us in a more profitable direction. Beyond current medical knowledge, but impinging more and more upon it, is the field of parapsychology, the findings of which cannot be ignored, notwithstanding all the scientific caution with which conservative scientists not unnaturally approach them. "Out of the body" experiences and other phenomena connected with the process of dying call for and are receiving close attention. Evidence is accumulating that leaves open-minded people in little doubt that the body we see, which we call fat or lean and tall or short, turning the scales at a certain weight, is not the only body we have.

To put the situation as cautiously as possible, much evidence suggests that (as has been for long held by the sages of other religions and in certain circles within the Christian Church) there is also a subtler body, a counterpart to the body we habitually talk about. There is in principle no reason why bodies might not be "made out of" finer stuff than are the tissues of the bodies with which we are familiar. Since these have turned out to be far more intricate than people took them to be right down to comparatively recent times, the notion that we might have a subtler "double" is not so far-fetched as it must have seemed to many a hundred years ago. It might be more like electricity, for instance, than water and fat. The common objection, that physicists have not so far detected its presence (not, at any rate, to the satisfaction of all), is not by any means fatal. The microscopic world could not have been detected till the invention of the microscope, nor the outer galaxies till the Palomar 200-inch telescope was built. There is at any rate an impressive corpus of serious literature on parapsychology to suggest certain possibilities.

If, as modern parapsychology indicates and as has been for centuries held in other religions, we do have what is sometimes called a "body of light" or "astral body" as well as the grosser one, and if this other body is capable of operating in some way by itself, retaining our energy in some way not presently known to us with the precision scientists insist upon, we may then ask certain special questions in the case of the body of Jesus Christ. Although in most of us little is ordinarily noticeable at death, beyond the cessation of breathing and certain other clinically observable or detectable occurrences such as *rigor mortis*, the energy in the body of an extraordinarily holy or spiritually vivacious person might produce much more striking phenomena. If Jesus Christ were indeed what Christian faith affirms him to be, the energy would presumably be so intensely strong as to produce a unique effect, such as the "melting" of the bones and tissues of the physical body as the "body of light" took over. This "body of light" might be so organized (presumably indeed it would be) that it would reflect the manner of his death: the imprint of the nails in the hands and feet and the wound in the side that convinced even the skeptical Thomas, according to the Gospel account. This would accord with certain reports by parapsychologists, such as Ian Stevenson, M.D., Carlson Professor of Psychiatry, University of Virginia, in cases of violent death.

Although the authenticity of the Holy Shroud that has been preserved at Turin since 1578 has not yet been either established or disproved, despite extensive recent investigations, some investigators have noted that *if* what happened was something such as has been suggested here, it might very well have produced the positive imprint, back and front, of a human body such as is to be found on that mysterious garment, together with the stigmata. For the present, this is of course speculative; nevertheless, it is noteworthy. In these matters we should explore all paths that show any reasonable promise, more especially if they relate to anything so central for Christians as the Resurrection of Christ. We should always be careful, of course, not to strain the evidence in any way.

Joachim Jeremias, Emeritus Professor at Göttingen and an internationally acclaimed New Testament scholar, rightly recognizes that any attempt to discover precisely what the appearances of the Risen Christ meant to the first witnesses seems at first sight hopeless. It would be difficult enough even with an ordinary event such as a street accident or a political uprising to tell what exactly had been experienced by various witnesses writing or speaking decades after the event they saw take place. As we have seen, nobody in the New Testament actually reports an eyewitness account of the Resurrection, only of the appearances of Jesus in his risen glory. Jeremias goes on, however, to make a hypothesis from what is known of the background and circumstances of the first Christians.

Judaism, he reminds us, knew nothing of any anticipated resurrection *as an event in history*. In all Jewish literature there is nothing like the account of the Resurrection as we have it in the Gospels and in Paul. Where stories of raising from the dead occur they are always stories of cures or resuscitations, as is the story of the raising of the daughter of Jairus in the Gospel. Resurrection to glory was always seen in Jewish literature, when it was seen at all, as the dawn of a new creation. The disciples, Jeremias then suggests, would be aware of a dawning of a new age, a turning point in history. He cites the remarkable passage in Matthew (27:51ff., JB), which contains a reference to the opening of graves and the raising of many bodies of saints who had fallen asleep. These resurrected saints, according to the account in Matthew, "came out of the tombs" after the Resurrection of Jesus, "entered the Holy City and appeared to a number of people." This is indeed a most remarkable passage. One recalls also the other occurrences reported at the death of Jesus: the tearing of the Temple veil and the earthquake, for example. Jeremias is surely right in asserting the confidence of the disciples that a new age had dawned. They were, they thought, witnessing the end of the age. We know that the Resurrection was closely connected in later tradition with the Ascension and Session at the right hand of God, which we shall consider in the next chapter, and there we clearly have the notion that the old dispensation was over and a new age begun that would give way in turn to the end of the world at the Second Coming. Yet, while Jeremias is convincing in the point he makes here, what he says does not at all exclude the proposal that the disciples and others were truly confronted with Jesus Christ in his risen glory. The interpretation I have suggested will surprise only those who are unfamiliar with parapsychological phenomena. To those who are, it will seem what one would expect it to seem, except of course for its peculiarly striking character, which no less is what any Christian believer would expect. If, moreover, we are talking of a unique case of something that happens all the time in a dimension of being beyond our own, even the Matthaean story of appearances in Jerusalem of various deceased holy men and women would seem by no means incredible.

Such appearances, if the proposal I am taking seriously should be true, would not be the appearances of "ghosts" or "spirits" as popularly understood. In popular imagination a ghost or spirit manifests himself or herself as a mere shadow of what the living reality has been. Ghosts lack the vitality of "real people." They are supposed to be made of a very tenuous, fluffy substance that is easily dispersed in air, like hoarfrost or a cloud. They speak, if at all, indistinctly. Though there are tales of green and other colored ghosts, most ghosts are gray silhouettes. By contrast, what Paul claims to have seen on the Damascus Road is a vision of blinding brightness, with whom he engages in a highly articulate conversation. Between what is popularly understood as a "ghost" and what is claimed about the appearances of Jesus Christ after the Resurrection lies an infinite gulf.

Consider the narrative of the discovery by Mary Magdalene (John 20:12, JB) that "two angels in white" were sitting, one at the head, one at the feet, of where Jesus had lain in the tomb. Angels are characteristic of Semitic lore and play a notable part in both Jewish and Islamic tradition; but the notion that two such "beings of light" should be so deployed in the tomb is highly significant. One recalls the strange painting by Léon Bonnat of the martyrdom of Saint Denis in the Panthéon, Paris. The severed head bears around it a halo of light; rays of light stream also from the trunk at the place where the head has been severed. This accords with an ancient way of expressing the luminosity of the "other body" or "astral double" so familiar both in the thought of antiquity and in contemporary parapsychological discussion. As we shall see when we come to discuss the concept of love (*agape*) in later chapters on the Holy Spirit and the Church, strong Christian tradition holds that the power of sacrificial love knows no barriers and surmounts all obstacles, not least physical ones. We have seen something of this in the last chapter. Christians who have experienced this power in those whom they love and by whom they are loved and who are at the same time open to ancient tradition and modern parapsychology will have little difficulty in seeing what the narratives are describing, and they will take very seriously the proposal that the disciples and others were indeed confronted with their Master in his risen glory.

After all, no sane person could conclude that the "end of the age" had come and that a new one had been already ushered in without any tremendous catalyst. A bereaved family may moan that the world will never be the same again because of the death of the beloved; but for them to conclude that the old order of things has passed and a new and infinitely better one is now begun would require something far more than the mere will to believe it. To suppose, as many biblical scholars tend to suggest, that the disciples and others who had loved Jesus conjured up an image of him in their brains and that, as a result of their fevered fancy, they announced that the only age known in the history of the world had come to an end and a new one had begun, is to postulate a more ridiculous psychological miracle than any wonder the New Testament records. It is also to tie oneself to a very mechanistic and outmoded way of thinking about the nature of the human body.

The Church traditionally celebrates Easter only after a long Lent of prayer and fasting, culminating in the elaborate penitential ritual of Holy Week and especially of Good Friday, when the altar is stripped bare, the tabernacle emptied, its door flung open, and the altar cross and other devotional objects covered with a black or violet cloth. All this helps to prepare the faithful to appreciate something of the joy of the Easter liturgy. But the richest understanding of Easter comes only to those who have known both Good Friday and Easter in their own lives and whose hearts, therefore, are always prepared to beat with Easter joy. This is the joy that is at the core of the Nicene Creed, to sing which with one's friends is one of the greatest delights of the Christian life. Those who know best what it reflects of the life of every Christian have rarely much difficulty in understanding what confronted the disciples and others when they saw and touched the Lord Jesus Christ in the luminosity of his risen glory.

Arraigned before the Great Sanhedrin, Jesus had answered the High Priest's question with the awesome words: *ani hu!*—"I am He!" (Mark 14:62). He had frequently used these words in the course of his ministry. For example, when the disciples saw Jesus walking on the lake as they rowed, they were afraid, thinking they had seen a ghost, and Jesus reassured them: "*Ani hu.* Don't be afraid!" (Mark 6:50; John 6:16ff.) This affirmation, "I am He," is often ambiguous. It could mean simply "It's me"; but it could also mean "I am the Eternal One." Certainly the phrase, which occurs over and over again in the Old Testament, is used as a theophanic formula: "I am He! I am the Lord your God!" (cf. Isa. 43:1ff.) The phrase was used liturgically at the Feast of the Tabernacles and had acquired a ritual significance: they are words for God to utter, not a human being. Jesus used them in ways that suggest so strong an echo of the liturgical, ritual use that we cannot easily resist the conclusion that he was using them pointedly to make the affirmation that was blasphemy to orthodox Jewish ears. The disciples must have heard it many times from his lips. They had walked in faith with their Master. Now all that was over. Now, when he appears to them in all the luminosity of his glory, he has no need to make the affirmation. At length they recognize him, and as he confronts them they need no *ani hu* and he gives them none, for they *know* it is the Lord. That is what Christians celebrate at Easter.

O God, whose blessed Son did manifest himself to his disciples in the breaking of bread; Open, we pray thee, the eyes of our faith, that we may behold thee in all thy works; through the same thy Son Jesus Christ our Lord. Amen.

—*Book of Common Prayer* (American, 1928),
Collect for Easter Monday

CHAPTER X

Ascension

and ascended into heaven,
and sitteth on the right hand of the Father

POPULAR iconography, in which Christ is depicted as rising from earth like a rocket or balloon in a perpendicular ascent into space, has no doubt been especially responsible for much foolish misunderstanding about the nature of that which Christians have from the earliest times celebrated as one of the great Feasts of the Church: the Ascension of Christ. While it is true that the Hebrews, in common with their Semitic neighbors, did have a primitive concept of heaven as a great vault covering the earth, we must not suppose that they or any other primitive peoples thought so simplistically as they often sound. Heaven, for them, was both a natural, astronomical phenomenon and a theological conception.

Only two New Testament texts present the Ascension of Christ as an historical event empirically observed: Luke 24:50f. and Acts 1:9f. Both use restrained language. Luke says only, "Now as he blessed them he withdrew from them and was carried up to heaven" (JB). Acts, which is the work of the same author, says: "As he said this he was lifted up while they looked on, and a cloud took him from their sight" (JB). One needs little training in literary matters to see that nothing here could justify the ridiculous notion that Jesus Christ rose up into the air like a rocket on its way to the moon. If I told you, as well I might, that I had seen the sun, in the late evening, fall into the Pacific Ocean, you surely would not suppose I meant that it had gotten wet. Even astronomers speak of the sun's rise, though they know very well that such language is an echo of a kind of astronomy that nobody has believed for about five hundred years. If I told you that I have seen the sun set more beautifully at Cape Sounion than in most other places, you would not suppose me to be scientifically antediluvian; at worst you would charge me only with a little sentimentality.

The more numerous texts relating to what the Creed affirms here either treat the Ascension as a theological truth or do not mention it at all. For instance, Christ was "taken up" in glory (I Tim. 3:16, JB), he sits "at the right hand of God" (Heb. 1:3, 13; 8:1; 12:2, JB) and God has "put everything under his feet" (Heb. 2:7-9; 10:12f., JB). Sitting at the right hand of God is a way of saying that he shares in the power of God in the administration of the world. Saying that God has "put everything under his feet" is likewise a way of affirming Christ's triumph. To suppose there is a throne on which God sits and that a side throne is provided for Christ on God's right would be as absurd as asking us to conclude that Christ's feet must be larger than the rest of the universe, since all things are under them.

One text is especially noteworthy: "He... ascended far above the heavens, that he might fill all things" (Eph. 4:10, RSV). That is a way of saying that Christ has gone beyond this "sky-and-earth" dimension of being and into another dimension. That there is such "another dimension" of being is not, of course, something that a physicist would account within his domain; but neither is any of the innumerable psychic phenomena familiar to us in everyday life, such as thought itself. Thought is certainly not something for physicists to consider (at any rate not in their working hours) though they operate in this dimension of being even while they do physics. Well-established psychic phenomena, such as telepathy and hypnotism, also belong to a dimension of being beyond the spatial one of earth and stars. Time itself is beyond the Euclidean space of three-dimensional geometry. So the proposal that the Risen Christ withdrew from this dimension of being in which our bodies are "spread out" in space and into another dimension need cause us no affront. On the contrary, it is surely precisely what one must say.

Nevertheless, some might object that we have treated the texts in Luke and Acts too cavalierly. After all, at least the account in Acts records that the disciples were actually "looking on" when "a cloud took him from their sight." This raises, of course, the question both of what they saw and of how it is related to what in fact happened. The answer must depend in part on what we take the nature of the Risen Body of Christ to be. If it was a manifestation of a "body of light," as has been suggested in the previous chapter, its "withdrawal" into a dimension beyond that of ordinary empirical observation is as one would expect. Luke himself records that the stranger on the road to Emmaus, whom the disciples eventually recognized as the Risen Christ, took bread, said the customary blessing, did the customary breaking, and then just as they recognized him he "vanished from their sight" (Luke 24:31, JB). Of course, a flash of light would carry their eyes upwards; of course, they would stand there gazing, momentarily half-blinded and psychologically stunned. The Luke-Acts record tells us what any good parapsychologist today would expect, given the circumstances recounted. Had the record intended a literalistic understanding, it would have gone on to tell us that the disciples saw the throne of God with Christ at the right hand, which of course they do not. Calvin noted nearly half a millenium ago that he could find nothing about *place* in Christ's "sitting at the right hand of God," but rather something about *function*. To see this he did not even need the revolution in science that quantum physics was to bring about some three hundred and fifty years later.

The Church has rightly emphasized throughout the centuries the importance of the doctrine of the Ascension. Christ, who companied with us during his earthly life, has transcended this earthly life of ours and, having accomplished his mission among us, has been "taken up" into a dimension beyond our ordinary ken. Only because Christian thought has for so long and so emphatically taken seriously the doctrines of the Incarnation and of the Resurrection could the doctrine of the Ascension have attained the role it has attained. It is a corollary of the rest. What is astonishing is that modern science and modern parapsychology make this doctrine more intelligible to us. It is an occasion for joyous celebration; it affirms the completeness of Christ's triumph. It is not merely a psychological triumph, not merely even a triumph for those human beings who have believed in Christ; it is a triumph of justice, an earnest of the Christian hope, which we are to deal with in the next chapter, that "Christ shall come again."

All this is very theological. It is about such realities that, not even if we had a photograph of what the disciples claimed they saw, could we produce any sort of scientific "proof." Despite all that some may say metaphorically about the Church as an extension of the Incarnation (a notoriously dangerous concept, beautiful though it be), the universal testimony of the Bible and of the Fathers of the Church is that the Incarnation was "for a season," and as it had a beginning in the mystery traditionally called the Virgin Birth, so it must have a clear and definite end. The Ascension marks the end. "Me ye have not always," warns Jesus (Matt. 26:11, KJV). God encamped with man only for a time, a very limited time, to provide the conditions for human salvation. The work he had to do had to come to an end.

The Ascension also calls to our attention another theological corollary. We are living in an interim period, between the First and the Second Coming of Christ. Ours is a special stage in human evolution: beyond the pre-Christian era yet "below" the age that is to be ushered in with the Second Coming. The Ascension marks the beginning of our era.

The temptation of the first-century Christians was, as we shall see in the next chapter, to expect this interim period to be short, perhaps only a few years or even a few months or days. We know better than that now. Although the ecological and other perils in the midst of which we live so alarm us as to make us wonder if the end of the present interim period is not now almost upon us, we have been accustomed, as the first-century Christians were not, to repeated warnings of the approach of a new order and the death of the present one. Those without Christian hope or any other assurance of the triumph of righteousness may well tremble at the fearful nuclear holocausts and other terrors that we all know may come upon us, for they can see nothing but final destruction for humankind as a result of such a cosmic catastrophe. Christians do share some of the same terror, for the end of humanity as we know it is not easy for anyone to contemplate; but the assurance Christians have of the ultimate triumph of justice and the final reign of love takes the fiercest sting out of the apocalyptic vision of an end to this world. Yet we must also accustom ourselves to the possibility that the present order may endure for thousands, perhaps even trillions, of years. For those spiritually gifted, the order beyond already impinges on ours; yet they, like the rest of us, know that it has not yet brought about the destruction of the present order of things and may take a very long time in doing so.

What came to the disciples must have been the sense of assurance that the Risen Christ was not simply a Being of Light coming repeatedly to console and strengthen them but that he had actually concluded his mission and was again "with God" whence he had come. The Ascension did not rule out further appearances. Paul's dramatic experience of the Being of Light, whom he met on the road to Damascus, is a striking example of such an encounter with the Risen and Ascended Christ (Acts 9). What the doctrine of the Ascension does is to leave us in no doubt that Christ, who truly encamped with us humans and after his terrible death uniquely overcame the limitations of human existence, being "raised from the dead," is now a cosmic reality with spiritual power beyond our wildest imaginings.

This doctrine is such that no kind of physics or chemistry could be relevant to it; it relates to the interior experience of the disciples and of every serious Christian, rather than to an observable event. Parapsychology, however, could be eminently relevant to the doctrine. That is by no means to suggest that it is a doctrine that reflects a "merely psychological" experience. On the contrary, it affirms, in line with all else that has been already said in the Creed, that God did his work in Christ so well that it is, in essentials, completed and that Christ *already* reigns "at the right hand of God" so as to be bringing about the transformation that will eventually manifest itself in the Second Coming.

Superficial commentators often remark that the world does not seem much improved since the First Coming. Such an observation often reflects either lack of historical knowledge or an outmoded anthropology or both. That there are many people today, and were in the last thousand years or more, whose qualities of mind and heart are of such an order as to have been either unthinkable or extremely rare before the time of Christ is undeniable. No one accustomed to weighing historical evidence could doubt it. The advance not only in human knowledge but also in human compassion and understanding is staggering. Such manifestations of a rise in the quality of human consciousness is not, of course, universal. It never was and there is no reason to suppose it ever will be: certainly not in the present world order.

To expect otherwise is possible only by thinking of the human race as an undifferentiated mass into which improvement can be stirred as one stirs pepper and salt into a pot of soup. Humanity consists, on the contrary, of individuals at a vast variety of stages of personal development, so that to complain that the world is not universally better than it was before the time of Christ is somewhat like complaining that a long-established school still has kindergarten classes and asking: should it not by this time have abolished everything below the twelfth grade? The vitality of a school is to be measured not by the ignorance of its novices but by the progress that some of them make as a result of the education they receive. A hospital is not to be judged by the mortality rate among those who come in with fatal diseases but, rather, by the recovery of those patients who have the will and self-discipline to profit from the institution's medical skill and nursing care.

Of course the question remains: is the advance in the quality of human consciousness attributable to Christianity? Might not it be as justly attributed to other religions that have been at work on our planet long before the time of Christ? Christianity certainly has no corner on holiness or learning, or on honesty or open-mindedness. On the contrary, one might argue that the Christian Church itself seems able to engender a disproportionately large number of wicked prelates and apostles of non-think.

These are all highly complex and disputable questions. It is well known that half a millenium after the time of Christ, at a time when China was at the height of its glory as one of the greatest civilizations the world had ever seen, Europe was a backwater, culturally, socially, and intellectually, with only a few monastic oases here and there across its wastelands. It is also true that a few centuries later, after the spectacular rise of Islam in the seventh century, the Muslim world so led the way in mathematics, medicine, and the sciences, that even Moses Maimonides, the greatest Jewish thinker of the Middle Ages, went to study at the Islamic seat of learning at Fez, as did also Gerbert of Auvergne (the future Pope Sylvester II), before the great European universities had been founded. For every Francis of Assisi, India could point to a Nanak, for every holy monk, a sadhu. More must be said on the relation of Christianity to other religions, when we come to the topics of the Holy Spirit and the Church. Meanwhile we should note two points.

The first is that no question of this kind could ever be settled statistically, sociologically, or by any of the standard methods or techniques used in the sciences. Our judgment on such questions must be based to a great extent on individual perception. The second point is that no educated Christian can fail to note either that the great humanistic renaissance of the fifteenth and sixteenth centuries, which has so revolutionized humane learning throughout the civilized world, was a profoundly Christian enterprise, or that the rise of modern science in the seventeenth century occurred in the matrix of Christendom. That is not to say that the Christian faith was necessarily the catalyst for either of these two tremendous human advances; but it is to assert that neither can be said to be in any way independent of the Christian climate in which they emerged. Christian art and literature are of such a high order and subtle quality that many have felt, as did Chateaubriand that the Christian faith can be shown by a study of history to have been the principal fountain of art, literature, and civilization in Europe, so that, even apart from the dogmatic claims the Church makes about the nature and mission of Jesus Christ, Christian faith is vindicated by its intellectual and spiritual fruits. Chateaubriand's contention, which he elaborated so beautifully in his great work, has been denigrated by many as a mere flotsam of the Romantic Movement of the early nineteenth century. It merits, I would suggest, more attention and respect than it has been generally accorded. For the Christian faith's stimulation of such a quality of art and literature, together with its cradling of modern science, though it could never "prove" the Incarnation or the Resurrection, is not insignificant; nor would any openminded Hindu or Buddhist, Jew or Sikh, be inclined to suppose it to be.

The Ascension is the Church's way of marking and celebrating the beginning of that stage of development, that order of existence, that kind of consciousness, that was made possible by the completion of Christ's work on earth. It was followed almost immediately by what happened at Pentecost, sometimes called "the Birthday of the Church," of which something more must be said in a later chapter. The traditional name for this event, "Ascension," is somewhat unfortunate, because it misdirects the imagination to a fanciful notion that has nothing to do with the theologically important fact to which our attention should be focused. The fact that nowhere in the writings of Paul is to be found even the most oblique reference to the Ascension as an historical event should apprise us that here we may more usefully consider theological and moral reality than historical or psychological occurrence.

One finds, among late medieval and Renaissance painters, the practice of combining the Resurrection and the Ascension as if they were one event. Examples of this are: Perugino (Pinacoteca, Vatican), Fra Angelico (Galleria Corsini, Rome), Piero della Francesca (Galleria Communale, Arezzo), Sodoma (Museo Nationale, Naples), and Verrocchio (a terracotta relief from Carreggi, now in the Museo Nazionale, Florence).[1]

GRANT, we beseech thee, almighty God, that the faithful members of thy Son may follow whither our Head and Prince has preceded us, through the same Jesus Christ our Lord.

—Leonine Sacramentary

1. My attention has been called to these examples by my friend and colleague, Susan Lenkey, Ph.D. (Budapest), Emerita Rare Book Librarian, Stanford University, and an art historian.

─────CHAPTER XI─────

Moral Reckoning

And he shall come again with glory
to judge both the quick and the dead:
whose kingdom shall have no end

THE belief that moral reckoning lies in store for all of us is common to most of the major religions of the world. In Christian thought it has always been envisioned as an end to the existing order of things and the ushering in of a new order by Christ, who in judging all of us will bring down the present order, with all its injustices, and establish a new order in which justice and righteousness shall prevail. Many have taken this to be an event that will occur on a particular day, attended by fearsome signs, such as a total eclipse of the sun, with blood and fire and smoke as portents of the coming of Christ in glory, enthroned in majesty as our divine Judge (Acts 2:19f.; cf. Joel 2:30f.). Others who have understood the Day of Judgment less literalistically have nevertheless expected a definite change in the order of things, however gradually brought about, in which Christ will cause justice to triumph over the forces of evil and injustice. However conceived, belief in the Second Coming of Christ is rooted in Scripture and persistent in Christian tradition. Scholars use the Greek word *parousia*, meaning "presence" or "arrival" (I Cor. 16:17; II Cor. 7:6f.; Phil. 1:26, 2:12) and used by Jesus in reference to the advent of the glorified Messiah, as the term to designate the Second Coming.

The first-century Christians expected the *parousia* to be

imminent; that is, it might happen any morrow, so they lived in constant expectation. Those who died were thought to be "asleep in the Lord" and would awaken any day to attend the Judgment that would terminate the present order and bring in the new one. On that day the sheep and the goats would be separated: terrible for the goats, unspeakably joyous for the sheep. The effect of this imminent expectation on first-century Christians was incalculably great. It affected their whole way of looking at their destiny, as we shall see in the last chapter of this book. There is no place for long-range planning when the present order is expected to end any day.

Gradually the imminence of the Second Coming diminished, but not the belief that there would be, sooner or later, an end to the present order. At various times the expectation of an imminent end has been revived among various groups, some of whom have also held that before the final Judgment Christ would reign for a long period, such as a thousand years, in a kingdom of his saints. Such groups based their teaching on the Book of Revelation, especially the twentieth chapter. Opinions of this kind were held here and there in the early Church but by the fourth century had lost much of their influence, which the more sophisticated views of Origen no doubt helped to diminish. Views of this kind, now technically called millenarian, were rare in the Middle Ages but reappeared in certain radical wings of the Reformation movement. They gained fresh currency later among the German Pietists, for instance, and in the English-speaking world among the Irvingites and Adventists.

Literalistic notions of this kind, especially about a particular day with the eclipse of the sun and other astronomical phenomena, are understandable in the first century, when the Christian Way was still new and Christians were being cruelly persecuted under Nero. The inner significance of the promise of Judgment had not yet sunk into the minds of Christians in the first flush of their expectancy. Nevertheless, their hope by no means turned sour. On the contrary, it mellowed. Though the sense of imminence receded, confidence in the Second Coming was undiminished. It remains a fundamental element in Christian belief to this day.

The question for us today is this: how are we to interpret the Christian hope expressed in this article of our faith? "He shall come again, with glory, to judge the living and the dead; whose kingdom shall have no end." To think of it in terms of a Dreadful Day, the Day of Wrath, with the accompaniments of fire and blood and thunderbolts, is to underestimate it. True, it is a moral reckoning and it is not yet; but we need not limit it to a day or an event of any kind. We must think of it, rather, in terms of the other fundamentals of the Christian faith that we have already been considering. Christ, through his resurrection, achieved victory over death, the supreme enemy of all who love life. It was certainly not a military or a political victory. It was the victory of love. Through the agony of Good Friday and the joy of Easter, Christ showed what sacrificial love can do, showed that that kind of love does really conquer all.

Yet Christ did leave his disciples. That is the inescapable implication of what the New Testament writers expressed in the story of the Ascension, according to which "he was taken up; and a cloud received him out of their sight" (Acts 1:9, KJV). The disciples had seen the tragedy and the glory in the life, death, and resurrection of their Master. Their hearts were ablaze with love of him, yet he was taken from them. Common sense dictated mourning; but love goes far beyond what common sense can tell us. Having seen the power of love, they knew its boundlessness. The "men" who "stood by them in white apparel" assured them that "Jesus, which is taken up from you into heaven, shall so come in like manner as ye have seen him go into heaven" (Acts 1:10f., KJV). Such is the confidence of love, for love knows its own stupendous power. Love "beareth all things, believeth all things, hopeth all things, endureth all things," Paul declared in his great celebration of the power of love (I Cor. 13, KJV) in which he affirmed the supremacy of self-emptying love over faith and hope, as well as over all knowledge. Love is the key to an understanding of the promise of the Second Coming of Christ.

Love bestows a unique *kind* of knowledge. When we have loved Christ so much that we have come to know him as a friend, as ever present with us, we know too (for it is given with that knowledge) that the presence we enjoy is but a token, an earnest of the fuller presence we are destined to enjoy. One of the mysteries of love is that it grows with the absence of the beloved. Such is the paradox of love that, when the beloved is physically absent, his or her presence is felt in a new and special way. In the words, "I miss you," is an announcement of that unique sense of presence that physical absence engenders. One must love deeply for this to happen. Everyone who has suffered the loss of a beloved husband or wife or even a close friend must learn in some measure how the anguish of such bereavement is accompanied by a profound sense of the presence of the beloved in a new mode of being. The disciples, having lost the physical presence of their Master and Lord, could not but soon learn that new dimension of the presence of Christ among them. With this new awareness, however, had to come also the recognition that this awareness was merely a prelude. The love they knew in their own hearts sprang from what they had learned of Christ's infinite love for his people and they understood, by the power of that love, that the Lord would show himself in an even fuller and more radiant presence in time to come.

The Christian hope is to see the glory of God. That is not a merely pious-sounding phrase. It is also anything other than a mere luxuriating in a delightful vision. To see the glory of God entails, among much else, seeing righteousness and justice prevail. Without such hope our faith would be unwarranted. In faith we believe in the ultimate triumph of God over the appalling injustices we see all around us, as well as the absurdities of political and social life. We say, in effect: so it is now and so it may be for long; but in the end there will be moral reckoning. To think of the moral reckoning crudely in terms of a cosmic Criminal Court with Jesus Christ on the Bench and Satan as District Attorney is not only primitivistic; such a picture grievously distorts the situation.

We should think not of Christ sitting in judgment but of Christ introducing conditions in which justice will be done. We reap what we sow. It may take a long time, longer perhaps than we are capable of conceptualizing; but in the end we shall gather the fruits of what we put into the soil. Christ has made the harvest possible; but what we have done with the possibilities is what we must expect. The faithful Christian, as he toils along life's path, knows that his toil is not in vain. His faith is that, bleak though the fields look now, they will yield in the long run fruit beyond all ordinary expectation. Without love he could know nothing of this. The knowledge comes with the assurance that only love can give.

One of the greatest manifestations of love is the willingness to accept forgiveness. When the seeds that we sow by our deeds are watered by a humility and love that is able to accept forgiveness for the wrongs we do, the effect of the wrongs melts like ice under a warm sun. Modern psychoanalysis has abundantly shown how this works. Though the law of moral reckoning is inexorable, an authentic love that seeks, through penitence, to accept forgiveness conquers all.

The Christian hope is that such love will so increase among us as to bring in, eventually, the new order of things, which we may interpret as a new stage in the evolution of humankind. What it is we do not profess to know, nor did anyone ever claim to know; but if it be better, what more can we ask?

The moral law of the universe, as Kant saw so well in his own way two hundred years ago, operates automatically. It is a causal principle. Kant was thinking in terms, of course, of the classical physicists of his day, and he rightly saw a striking parallel: the moral law works in its way very much as the so-called "laws of physics" work in theirs. Kant was right. He was enunciating what the ancient Hebrew lawgivers and prophets saw so well in their way. As they put it, the Lord avenges wickedness and makes righteousness in the end prevail. Christian faith, with its emphasis on forgiveness and grace, seemed to many not to fit such an understanding of the moral law. Let us see whether it is as ill-fitting as it looks.

W. Heisenberg discovered and formulated a principle that is characteristic of modern quantum physics. According to this principle, for any two canonically conjugate magnitudes, such as position and momentum, or time and energy, only one can be measured to any degree of accuracy. An increase in the precision of the measurement of one magnitude is accompanied by a proportional decrease in the precision of the measurement of the other. When one magnitude is ascertained with absolute accuracy, the other remains no less absolutely indefinite. The world picture given us in quantum mechanics is nevertheless deterministic in its own way. The difference lies in the fact that the uncertainty in the prediction of occurrences in the sense world is reduced to an uncertainty in translating the symbols of the world picture into the sense world and those of the sense world into the world picture. In other words, there is no less certainty than in the old classical mechanics, but it is in a greater dimension, in which the operation of the laws is not so easily apprehended. Three-dimensional chess operates by the same basic principles as ordinary chess; but for most of us those principles are much less easily perceived. Now this is very much what Jung's analytical psychology has to say of the laws of the psyche. They are not discernible by the senses, as are, say, the gravitational laws of classical physics. Indeed, at first encounter they do not seem discernible at all. Nevertheless, they operate no less surely. So the new order that Christians expect Christ to usher in works no less certainly than an "eye for an eye, tooth for a tooth" law, though it is the law of love. To put the matter as simply as possible, love has its own laws, and though the certainty of their operation is more difficult for most of us to discern than is that of the more external kind of laws to which we are more habituated, the certainty is there, at the heart of all things. Christ came not to destroy the Torah with the gospel (Matt. 5:17). The law of love works no less surely than Kant's moral law of duty.

So the triumph of love over our present order and the ushering in of the new age, the kingdom of God, for whose coming we pray, is properly called Judgment. We are to remember only that God's judgment operates according to the law of his own Being, which is the law of love. So the ancients and the medieval people were right in pronouncing the Judgment to be terrible: *dies irae,* the day of wrath. For to be faced with the operation of the law of love before we are ready for it is more fearsome than any other punishment we could conceive. We are thereby automatically excluded from what is going on. It might be imagined as somewhat like being suddenly let loose in graduate school with a high school or even a kindergarten mind. Even God cannot forgive us when we cannot forgive ourselves, and a heart that does not know the measure of the sacrifice that authentic love entails is even more incapable of self-forgiveness than of the forgiveness of others.

The kingdom that Christ is to usher in is said in the Creed to have "no end." Many of us are inclined to envision that as a state of unchangeableness, a static life, which is a self-contradiction, for life by its very nature is dynamic and the law of love is assuredly not going to diminish the dynamism of life; it must, of course, enhance it. When the Nicene Fathers said of the kingdom that is to

come that it is "without end" (*ouk estai telos*), they meant something very different. What such a notion must mean to us, with
our knowledge of the evolutionary principles of life itself, is an
order of being into which we are to enter that will bring about in us
an irreversible advance in our consciousness and in our apprehension of the Being of God. The point will be reached (tomorrow or
trillions of years hence) at which the present state of humanity will
be a state of the past. Humanity as we know it will be extinct, as
now are the sabre-toothed tiger and the dodo. Another order will
supervene: we may call it superhuman if we wish, but at all events
it will make the present order of humanity obsolete. Those who by
that time are unable to cope with that new order in which love
prevails will have, so to speak, nowhere to go. They will be like the
last dinosaur on the day that dinosaurs were doomed. So the
"day" of Judgment is not inappositely called "Doomsday," since
for some it will be just that. But for those who will be able to cope
with an order in which Christ reigns, having established a kingdom of love in which men and women need the dispositions necessary for survival in such an order, the new and fuller life they will
enjoy will be an unspeakable bliss. They will know, too, that the
state they have attained is irreversible. It is theirs unconditionally.
It can have no end. Yet it cannot be that there is no advancement,
for that would mean, even in such a glorious state, not life but the
stultification that leads to death, while Christ's reign, on the contrary, means superabundant life.

Modern scientific thought, far from making such a notion
less credible, makes it much more so. Here we are better off than
the ancients, for they did not know that what was being promised
had happened already on a much lower level, when man, the
thinker, first emerged. We know this, so it is not so difficult for us
to see how it must all happen again at a higher level if, as we have
postulated (as does the Creed at the outset), that at the core of the
universe God rules in love.

When we talk of the Christian hope, we think of individual
salvation, the future life that is promised to each individual who
accepts Christ and does the will of God. Of this complex and
especially difficult subject more must be said in the last chapter
when we take up the question of "the life of the world to come."
But all that could ever be said on that subject would be meaningless

without the concept of moral reckoning to which this present chapter has been devoted. For a Christian's belief in a future and fuller life is grounded in his or her belief in a God whose acts are such as the Bible describes and whose Being is such as the Church worships and proclaims. Without such a prior belief, a Christian's hope for a future life of any kind would be indeed a pipe dream. As Paul eloquently affirms, only because of the resurrection of Christ dare we hope for our own resurrection.

Without the doctrine of moral Judgment no authentic Christian belief could be vindicated. Indeed, the most notoriously difficult kind of question for the Christian is the one posed by Job: "Wherefore do the wicked live, become old, yea, are mighty in power?" (Job 21:7, KJV). In the last resort, the answer to this question is that the wicked shall not prosper forever nor the righteous forever groan under the burden of injustice and the yoke of suffering. Unless there is moral reckoning, hope of a future life is out of the question, for God would not have honored his promise. The very basis for our faith would collapse. To rejoice in the Second Coming is an integral part of a Christian's faith. The instinct of popular devotion has been right in emphasizing the Day of Judgment. Traditional understanding of the nature of that Judgment, however, has done less than justice to its splendor, not usually through anyone's fault or neglect, but for lack of the knowledge we enjoy today. Through a new vision of the nature of the Second Coming we can see more clearly the grandeur of the Christian drama and probe a little better into the depths of the love of God.

Although prediction of any kind is always hazardous, since there are so many imponderables, some circumstances in our present world situation should not be overlooked. While we cannot say categorically that our planet might not go on for a very long time, perhaps trillions of years, the possibility of a comparatively speedy end cannot seem in the least remote to anyone acquainted with the ecological facts today. The danger from the use of nuclear weapons is too obvious to need comment. The human population explosion and the excessive consumption of energy are hardly less well known as portents of disaster. Yet all these, however grave, may not be insurmountable obstacles to the continuation of life on our planet. More startling and less well known is the fact that the earth's stock of living things is in any case being depleted at a remarkable rate.

A few years ago a population biologist at the University of California told a meeting of conservationists at La Jolla that half a billion years of animal evolution are coming to a halt, that the world is in the midst of a "biological holocaust without precedent," and that the evolution of vertebrates in the tropics will cease by the end of the present century. By this he did not mean that *all* animals are to become extinct by then, though a million species (from large mammals to small insects) will; but, for lack of space, tropical mammals will stop evolving; that is, they will stop changing their genetic traits as they do very slowly by the trial-and-error process of what has hitherto been accounted "normal evolution." Animal populations are diminishing from starvation and disease at unprecedented rates. Forests are being cut down extensively. The most important evolutionary changes have occurred through the process of speciation by which two or more groups of animals of the same species become separated from one another over lengthy periods, sometimes as a result of natural barriers such as mountains and rivers. Many biologists predict that, with the cramming of animals into a few areas in the tropics, the novelty in nature will be extinguished and speciation will come to an end, with grave results. Add to all this the natural catastrophes that occur but that were less devastating when the animal population was spread over larger areas, and it is easy to see how suddenly an entire species could be eliminated. That a million species in the tropics may die in a decade or two is an alarming prediction when one considers that nine-tenths of all species live in the tropics. A million represents, at a very rough estimate, something like fifteen per cent of all the species in the world. If many animals do overcome those odds, they still will stop evolving.

Many anthropologists believe that the physical evolution of humankind has come to an end; that is to say, human beings are not going to go through any further modifications of the kind that long ago enabled them to talk and to walk upright. Geneticists predict that in just over a century one child in ten may be born with a serious genetic defect, such as muscular dystrophy. On the other hand, the human brain has an immense capacity for further development. If humanity does survive on this planet, what, then, will be the nature of its survival?

Nothing in all this means that the world is necessarily soon coming to an end. Nevertheless, there are pointers that do suggest to a Christian that we *may* be witnessing the signs that the New Testament says are to precede the Second Coming of Christ. To any educated person who believes in the Second Coming at all, its imminence cannot be easily ruled out.

MAKE us vigilant and careful, O Lord our God, in expecting the coming of thy Son Christ our Lord; that when he shall come knocking he may find us not sleeping in sin but wakeful and rejoicing in his praise; through the same Jesus Christ our Lord.

—Gelasian Sacramentary,
Collect for Advent

CHAPTER XII

He Who Gives New Energy

And I believe in the Holy Ghost,
The Lord and Giver of Life,
Who proceedeth from the Father [and the Son],
Who with the Father and the Son
together is worshipped and glorified,
Who spake by the Prophets.

GHOST, in the beautiful antique language of the traditional English version of the Creed, is the robust native Saxon word that our English-speaking forefathers preferred to the imported Latin equivalent, *spirit.* The history of the Christian doctrine about the Holy Spirit is long and its biblical roots complex. Not all of it would be directly relevant to our needs here; but some background is helpful in understanding some of the contemporary issues.

The Hebrew word is *ruach,* which means simply "wind" or "breath" and is onomatopoeic, mimicking the sound of that to which it refers. The Greek counterpart, used in the New Testament, is *pneuma,* which has a similar background and is the word from which we get, for instance, *pneumatic* as applied to tires, balloons, and the like. It is grammatically neuter. Even in early biblical literature we read of the action of the *ruach* of God. Not only was it that which made Adam into a living being; we read (Exod. 35:30f.) that the artistic skill of Bezaleel was inspired by the divine *ruach.* The message of the prophets was definitely inspired by that same Spirit (Isa. 61:1f.). In later Hebrew literature, intellectual and artistic gifts in general were seen more and more as gifts of the Spirit of God. Finally Wisdom (in Greek *sophia*, which is grammatically feminine, by the way) comes to be so closely associated with the Spirit of God (Wisd. of Sol. 7:7, 9:17; Ecclus. 39:6) as to be personified and almost identified with that Spirit. Such developments are not without their counterparts in pagan religion, where literary and artistic inspiration is seen as coming from a god or goddess, such as one of the Muses. In ancient Roman religion, each man had his Genius and each woman her Juno. But in the Bible such inspiration is seen as coming directly from the Spirit of the One God.

The notion of the action of the Spirit in the Old Testament is interesting, not least because it is so plainly distinguishable from the characteristically Hebrew concept of God's acting in history. That God acts in history was a basic presupposition of Hebrew thought; but on the whole God is represented as acting by fiat, by decree. As we recall from our earlier discussion, God and Nature are not distinguished in ancient Hebrew thought. God could and did occasionally send plagues unexpectedly or strike down an enemy warrior or king. This concept of the act of God survives in our legal language today: insurance policies, for instance, may exclude from coverage what are traditionally called acts of God, such as storms and earthquakes. In modern usage this is a technical phrase that generally means inevitable accidents due directly and exclusively to natural causes, not human intervention of any kind, and which it would be unreasonable to expect a person to be able to foresee or prevent. In primitive Hebrew thought, generally speaking, God did not move among his people or directly participate in their affairs. The notion of the movement of the Spirit directing the thoughts of prophets and inspiring the work of artists is distinctive.

This is the theme that is further developed in the New Testament and in later Christian tradition. The Spirit of God comes upon Mary, and she conceives the Christ. So special does the Spirit of God become that Jesus warns his hearers that, while all other sin is forgivable, sin against the Spirit of God is not (Mark 3:19). In John the Spirit becomes *ho paraklētos*, the Paraclete or Advocate, who helps, guides, counsels, and strengthens the People of God. The Apostles are said to have received direct communication from the Spirit (Acts 11:12, 16:6f.), who also participated in their deliberations (Acts 15:28) and who, through the Apostles, was conveyed to others (Acts 8:15f., 19:6). In Paul's thought the Spirit plays an important role. He describes the fruits of the Spirit of God in men and women (Gal. 5:22f.). We are to treat our bodies with respect, for, Paul tells us, they are the Temples of the Holy Spirit (I Cor. 6:19; cf. II Cor. 6:16). Except for the second and third letters of John, every book in the New Testament mentions the Holy Spirit. The most dramatic action of the Spirit of God recorded in the New Testament is, of course, the Spirit's descent on those who were assembled on the day of Pentecost (Acts 2).

Nevertheless, the notion that the Holy Spirit is a distinct *hypostasis* or "person" of the Godhead is a much later development. No first-century literature addresses the Spirit as God. Tertullian and the Montanists in the second century do have a special doctrine of the Holy Spirit. The subject was, however, an open one till comparatively late. From about 360 onwards, much theological controversy attended the question of the Holy Spirit's divinity. East and West were divided over it for centuries. Some denied the divinity of the Holy Spirit as others denied the divinity of Christ.

In the end the Great Schism between Constantinople and Rome in 1054, which still splits the Greek and Roman Churches, was (though it had a long and more complex background) officially about that question. To many of us today it may seem an extraordinarily technical, not to say nitpicking, point to bring about so historic and lasting a division in the Christian Church; but in the medieval context in which the controversy had raged it was indeed of great importance. The question was this: does the Holy Spirit proceed from the Father only (as the Greeks held) and not from the Son, or may we say that the Holy Spirit proceeds from both? When at last the Roman Church added the word *filioque* ("and the Son") to the Nicene Creed, the Greeks vehemently denounced the addition, and not without reason: it was not part of the original text of the Creed and, though it had become a disputed point, the Greeks regarded it as both heretical in itself and symbolic of the corruption of the West.

The West, however, had by no means universally approved the controversial addition. Indeed, when Charlemagne, who had been crowned at Rome on Christmas Day, 800, by Pope Leo III, had wanted to have the change adopted, Leo, though he personally favored it, did not wish to offend the Greeks, so he deposited the

Creed in its original form in two silver tablets at the tomb of Peter. The controversial addition continued to be widely used, however, and soon after the year 1000, it was used in Rome, precipitating the Great Schism.

Though important theologians in the West from Augustine (*De Trin.*, XV, 26, 27) onwards have defended the *filioque* (notably E. B. Pusey in 1876), the Greeks' theological arguments (not least the classic ones of the Cappadocian Fathers) against what came to be called the "Double Procession" are formidable and, I think, persuasive. The *filioque* addition is nowadays omitted from many modern versions of the Creed in the West. I have enclosed it in square brackets, if only because it is not in the Greek text, which is also provided. The issue is not trivial and represents, many of us think, another instance of how the subtleties of Greek thought tend to be lost in translation.

Even by the time the Nicene Creed was formulated, the role of the Holy Spirit was still an open question. That the Spirit is a mighty force, an inexhaustible field of energy in the Household of Faith, has never been in dispute; but whether it is proper to identify the Spirit with God was still not entirely settled when the Creed was formulated. So the Creed, while not going so far as to state explicitly that the Spirit is "in the Godhead," does affirm that the worship we give to the Father and to the Son is to be given also to the Spirit.

Whatever we may think of the ways in which such technical controversies developed in the past, all Christians will concur in the universal testimony of the Church that the Spirit is the bearer of *phōs, zoē,* and *agapē* (light, life, and love). Yet it is not to be supposed that wherever there is any kind of light and life and love the Holy Spirit is directly at work. What the Church has always contended is that wherever the Holy Spirit is at work a special *kind* of light, a special *kind* of life, and a special *kind* of love emerges, changing those upon whom its influence falls. The Spirit lights an inextinguishable fire in the depths of our being. When that fire catches at the core of our being, it sets us ablaze with the love of God, and as we pass among other men and women, we transmit sparks of that fire that may likewise catch in them and so inflame them.

The obvious question about all that must surely be this: how can one tell whether the fire that is lighted in us and that we may be able to light in others because of it is authentic? There are so many fires lighted within us. It seems easy enough to recognize the fires of ambition, the fires of sexual passion, the fires of revenge, and to know that none of these is the fire of the Holy Spirit of God. But fires assume many guises, and we have an infinite capacity for self-deception. Among so many fires that warm and cheer and excite us, how can we discern this one fire that comes straight from the heart of God? Plainly, not everyone who yells "Pentecost" at you or croons "Holy Spirit" in your ears has been touched by the Breath of God; yet some fakes do look uncannily genuine. How can we tell which comes straight from "the Lord and giver of life"?

From early times, the work of the Holy Spirit has been so closely connected with the notion of the Church as the Household of Faith and the Unique Instrument of God that the Fathers generally have talked of the Spirit as to be found only in the Church. Yet according to John, Jesus said, "the wind [*to pneuma*] blows wherever it pleases; you hear its sound, but you cannot tell where it comes from or where it is going. That is how it is with all who are born of the Spirit (*ek tou pneumatos*)" (John 3:8, JB). Paul provides a test. If you are guided by the Spirit, he tells the Galatians, you will be free, yet you will not be thereby led into self-indulgence, which is the opposite of the work of the Spirit. The results of self-indulgence are obvious: fornication, fighting, envy, bad temper, and the like. What the Spirit brings is very different: love, joy, peace, patience, kindness, goodness, trustfulness, gentleness and self-control. After specifying these fruits of the Spirit of God, Paul concludes: "You cannot belong to Christ Jesus unless you crucify all self-indulgent passions and desires" (Gal. 5:13-24, JB).

We must surely also bear in mind that not everything that happens to be psychologically beneficial is to be hailed as the *direct* action of the Spirit of God. Whatever that action is, it is something unique. It infuses those who receive it with the living holiness of God. No one who disparages even the feeblest and most awkward gropings of beginners in the spiritual way can have been touched by the flame that the Breath of God fans into a blaze of holiness, for an indispensable mark of the Spirit's action is a unique magnanimity of heart and mind. The more men and women are set apart by the Holy Spirit, the less exclusive they are in their dealings with other people, especially fledglings in the Faith.

Since God is at least personal, whatever he is besides, his Spirit must be at least personal too. In the process of biological evolution, a knowledge of which has revolutionized our approach to all problems relating to the development of humankind, we may see the Spirit of God leading and organizing it from inside until at length the spirit of humankind emerges within the evolutionary process. Only so can the divine community, the Church, be gathered together. This divine community is the special locus of the action of the Holy Spirit; but the Spirit of God can know no bounds.

If we look at the ancestry of man we find a proliferation of species that begins to cease as the evolutionary movement passes to the higher simians. An increasing convergence takes place, issuing in the emergence of the self-conscious species we call man. It is at this point that evolution undergoes a fundamental change. Hitherto the process has borne man's ancestors along; now humankind, in the attainment of self-awareness, turns in upon itself. The self-consciousness of the human species, in which thought becomes possible, is a tremendously important turning point in the evolutionary process. Humanity takes over a great measure of its own development and growth. Nevertheless, more is needed for the attainment of the next step, which humanity cannot reach on its own. It is here that the divine energy, moving directly through the paths of men and women, fills them with a new capacity. That Spirit who "spake by the prophets" prepared humankind for a higher consciousness that propels it gradually toward the next stage in its destiny.

If the divine energy that is the action of the Spirit were to pass through humankind in the fulness of its power, it would destroy all whom it touched. So as God in becoming human had to fit his stature to our need, as we saw when discussing the self-emptying principle, so in pouring out his Spirit upon his Church, the People of God, he metes out only what we can take and use. This is often meager. Moreover, God's Spirit, as immanent in the paths we humans tread, must blow, as Jesus told his disciples, "where it pleases," and in ways far beyond the channels one might

expect. If the results of the Spirit's health-giving, life-giving fire
are visible in one out of a thousand of those over whom it blows,
the divine work has been done.

When we speak of life we are covering an enormous range in
evolutionary development. Here are some algae, which belong to
the lowest division of the vegetable world, having a relatively
simple structure and reproductive arrangement. They are very
diverse, ranging from unicellular organisms through various colo-
nial types to filamentous forms and then on to large growths such
as some seaweeds. They are alive, you truthfully say; but if I were
to rejoin, "You mean like my friend who received the Nobel Prize
last year?" you would probably laugh, and rightly too, for the
difference is not like the difference between a grain of dust and the
Empire State Building; it is a difference of quality. No aggregation
of algae, however vast, could make a man or even a mouse. But
then no number of elephants could make a man, not even the
village idiot. Again, the difference is qualitative. So when we call
the Holy Spirit the Lord and giver of life, we must include in some
way this enormous range, yet the kind of life with which we are
chiefly concerned when we talk of the Holy Spirit in the Church is
a quality of life so high that most of us are only beginning to attain it and many of us have not even begun. As to this "life
of the Spirit" that we Christians talk about, we are mostly at the
stage that humankind was at many thousands of years ago with
respect to the capacity to conceptualize and utter speech, when our
distant ancestors made their first halting attempts to think and
speak. Moreover, we need not go nearly so far down the scale as to
the algae to see an enormous difference in quality of life. We can
see it within humanity itself: the difference between a Schweitzer
or a Mother Teresa, on the one hand, and a drunken oaf, on the
other, is staggering.

The Holy Spirit opens our eyes and breaks our fetters so that
we may look at what God is doing and what we need to do and so
that we may arise in freedom and do it. Only through the outpouring of the divine energy among the first Christians could they have
even noticed the tremendous significance for humankind of the
Incarnation and Resurrection of Christ. To say that the Holy Spirit
acts in the Church is one thing, however; to say that the Holy
Spirit acts *only* in the Church would be quite another. In no way

can the Spirit's action be so limited. We rightly expect to find the Holy Spirit in the Church; but we should certainly not be right if we expected not to find the Spirit elsewhere. If wicked men or women shut the sluice gates against the Spirit in the Church, that same Spirit will break forth elsewhere as surely as water, when blocked, will spill out into rivulets and gorges. The Church, as Rufus Jones in his day reminded us, owes a large debt to heretics.

The one specific title the Creed gives to the Holy Spirit is Lifegiver. The Spirit vivifies that which is lifeless and restores to life that which is moribund. It is significant that the Spirit of God seems so often to work on the fringes of the Church, in the narthex rather than the nave. That is at least partly because the Church has legalistic, institutional, hierarchical aspects that, inevitable though they are, sap the life of the Church. To the superficial observer, these aspects constitute the Church and therefore seem to represent the places one must look to see what sort of life the Church has. In reality, however, they are the last places to look, since whatever authentic restoration and renewal sweep over the Church from time to time in its long history begin almost always in unexpected nooks and crannies, byways and outskirts, rather than in what would seem to be the more obvious places. Most of the great Orders of men and women (the Franciscans are a notable example) sprang up unexpectedly and before long were infusing new life into the Church. Sometimes, indeed, the most strange and aberrant heresies are, if only indirectly, harbingers of the action of the Holy Spirit on the Church. Nothing in the work of the Holy Spirit is predictable except its unpredictability.

The more we love the Household of Faith, the Christian fellowship that is the Church, the more clearly we see in it so much that is dead that should be superlatively alive, so much that is sick that should be healthy, so much that is stale that should be fresh. Great is the temptation to beat new life into the Church by borrowing techniques from the business world, by introducing novelties in ritual, or by simply introducing more animal energy into the Church's worship and assemblies. But that is as ineffective as trying to cure arthritis with a witch doctor's poultice. Nothing less than the direct action of the Holy Spirit can ever vivify that which is so petrified. Only the Breath of God can breathe new life into that which is crying out in suffocation. Yet many even among the most devout of Christians who are diligent in their prayers to God and who claim to love their Saviour Jesus Christ sorely neglect to pray to the Holy Spirit to pour into the Church the lifegiving energy that only he can provide.

The unique quality of life the Spirit of God brings is inseparable from the love (*agapē*) that comes with it, which is both deeply personal and suprapersonal. It is through the outpouring of this unique love that the Spirit, who is the "Spirit of truth," guides us "into all the truth" (John 16:13, RSV). The truth (*alētheia*) is not a truth that can be encompassed by the intellect alone, like a mathematical theorem or the function of oxygen in the bodies of mammals; it can be apprehended only by the whole of our being under the influence of the Holy Spirit. The work of the Spirit is not rapacious. The Spirit of God does not take possession of a man or woman by force. That would be a kind of spiritual rape. Perhaps evil spirits can sometimes so take possession of a human being in such a way as to call for exorcism; but one has only to recall the fruits of the Spirit of God to see that such qualities are valueless except to the extent that they inhere in a free being. The Holy Spirit, far from diminishing my freedom, enhances it. The spontaneity engendered in me is *my* spontaneity. I become more of an individual, not less. Far from providing me with an escape hatch, a back door out of the reality of my existence, the Spirit confronts me with it. Above all I attain an openness of heart and mind that only love (*agapē*) can give me. This love, which is the greatest of all gifts (I Cor. 13:13), also opens me in a special way to others into whom the new life is also being infused. The fellowship of the Spirit comes in the community of faith, though also in a more general way to all humankind. Because of the action of the Spirit of God I attain to a new dimension of being. I am making a new evolutionary leap into a higher consciousness that is transforming me radically and irreversibly.

This does not mean that I am "irreversibly saved," for I might turn away from God and destroy myself. This must always be possible. It was possible, according to Luke, even for the highest of the angels, Lucifer. It must always be possible for a free being, for that is part of what freedom entails. The fire of the Spirit may be quenched (I Thess. 5:19). Yet as a mammal who has attained the intellectual power to think and to speak, to laugh and to weep, can never go back to being a monkey or a dog, even if he so wished, so no one who has been touched by the action of the Spirit of God can go back to being anything less than that new and higher being into which he or she has been transformed.

THY blessed Unction from above
Is comfort, life, and fire of love.
Enable with perpetual light
The dulness of our blinded sight.

—Veni Creator, attributed to Rabanus Maurus
(probably ninth century)

CHAPTER XIII

One Catholic and Apostolic Church

And I believe one Catholick and Apostolick Church

EXCEPT for the word *God*, no word in the Creed is more confusingly ambiguous than the word *Church*. The confusions are of more than one kind, some trivial, some crucially important. We all speak habitually of the church as the building round the corner that some attend, as Jews attend a synagogue and Muslims a mosque. Then we also speak of "The Church of Sweden" or "The Dutch Reformed Church" or "The Roman Catholic Church," in which case we are thinking of an entire institutional organization. In the former case we should write the word without a capital letter, and in the latter we should use one. If the ambiguity went no further than that, no problem would exist; but in fact the ambiguities are labyrinthine, as anyone who has attended a serious ecumenical discussion must have noticed.

For instance, when a Roman Catholic, in conversation with a Methodist, talks of "your church" and "my church" he may mean by the former "The Free Methodist Church of North America" or "The Cumberland Methodist Church," but he is more likely to mean "Methodist churches in general," and he is not at all unlikely to be referring to "Protestant churches in general," and to be including, incidentally, several bodies (Lutheran and Anglican, for instance) not all of whose members readily so designate themselves. A Greek monk on Mount Athos, if he talked about "your church" at all, would very possibly include in it everything from the Old Order Amish Mennonite Church and the Church of England to the Roman Catholic Church and the Two-Seed-in-the-Spirit Predestinarian Baptists. At a much higher level of theological literacy, however, the ambiguities are even more troublesome. Many of the bitterest controversies in the history of Christianity have been about the nature of the Church more than they have ever been about faith and works or the abuse of indulgences. As I showed in *Corpus Christi* many years ago,[1] this is notably true of the Reformation, at the heart of whose controversies lay special understandings of the nature of the Church.

The concept of the Church is familiar to anyone reading the New Testament. The New Testament writers, indeed, presuppose the existence of the Church, if only because there were communities of Christians living and worshipping together before Paul went on his missionary journeys. Paul's use of the word *ekklesia* shows that he was thinking of its Hebrew original, "the congregation," the gathering together of the people of God in a particular place. Paul uses the phrase "the Body of Christ" to designate the oneness of the Risen Christ with the manifold communities in which he is adored. In this mystical vision of the Church, it has only one Head, Jesus Christ, the Head of the Body. Enormous difficulties have arisen and acrimonious controversies have been engendered, however, in the interpretation of such early Christian teaching about the nature of the Church.

The most profound theologians, including Augustine, have seen that the Church goes much further back than the coming of Christ. It was already there in some form in ancient biblical times, wherever righteous men and women adored God and sought to live aright in accordance with the divine will. We must indeed go further even than that, for the Church is already implicit in the action of God as Creator. As soon as creatures appropriate the freedom given them potentially in creation, they freely unite themselves in love with others who are using their God-given freedom by seeking truth, living rightly, and worshipping the

---

1. *Corpus Christi: The Nature of the Church according to the Reformed Tradition* (Philadelphia: Westminster Press, 1958).

Source of their free being, which is God. The "People of God" extend to the earliest times and are to be found all over the world and, for all we know, on other planets in distant galaxies.

The Christian Church, then, emerges as a new understanding of what it means to be the People of God, the Household of Faith. "Unto us a Child is born." We are the New Israel. Yet in spite of the dramatic novelty of our situation, we are still part of the evolutionary spiral that is leading all humankind into a new and greater dimension of being. Nevertheless, we claim to be "a new creation." We are "in Christ." We do have a special mission. Sociologists analyze the workings of the Church and sometimes dismiss it glibly; but all Christians, even in their most extreme exasperation with the Church, know how much more it is than a social phenomenon.

The Christian Church is what it is because of the Incarnation. It is sometimes called, rightly but misleadingly (for the concept is a dangerous one), an "extension of the Incarnation." Notwithstanding, the Incarnation, in one way or another, is still going on in the Church, however it has been fundamentally accomplished in the coming of Christ. For the work of Christ and the Holy Spirit of God goes on, raising men and women up to a new dimension of being. It is God that works in them, providing the conditions for their sanctification.

Some theologians express the nature of the Church, the Body of Christ, in the traditional distinction between the Church on earth (the Church Militant), the Church beyond the veil of death (the Church Expectant), and the Church in oneness with God (the Church Triumphant). Another perhaps even more important way of specifying the nature of the Church is that of distinguishing the Church from the kingdom of God. The Church represents a tremendous leap into higher consciousness; but it also posits yet a further stage to which the Church is always pointing: the kingdom of God, in which God's people will have totally subjected themselves to the reign of God's love. The kingdom is not yet realized; but the Church is an earnest of its coming.

Traditionally, a close mystical connection exists between the Church and the Eucharist. In a dramatic sermon, Augustine told his congregation that, when the priest gives them the Holy Communion, and when they respond to the words "The Body of

Christ" with the customary "amen," they must strive to *be* the Body of Christ, so that their "amen" may be true. The whole action of the Church is "for" the Eucharist, and the Eucharist can have no meaning apart from the Church. The Church is also associated with Mary as the vehicle of God. She, and therefore womanhood through her, mystically represent the Church. "He cannot have God for his Father," writes Cyprian in the third century (echoed by many, including Calvin in the sixteenth), "who has not the Church for his Mother." The Church, so understood, is the Mother of all Christians, and Mary is the Mother of our Lord. The priest, standing at the altar in the midst of the people in the central act of Christian worship, stands in the place of Christ; but, though what he does in Christ's name is stupendous, he is acting only in, through, and for the Church, our Mother. So profound is this symbolism in the Christian Church that all attempts to revamp it are doomed to failure and can produce nothing but schism or worse.

Many people today are not equipped, emotionally or intellectually, to grasp such a mystical interpretation of the divine drama. Yet there is no other way, for the drama is all of a piece. If halfway through *Hamlet* you turn Hamlet into Ophelia, or if halfway through *King Lear* Lear should become one of his children, you cannot but ruin the play, whether the leading part be played by Gielgud or a local boy trying out his talent. There are many ways of doing Shakespeare and certainly many ways of showing forth the function of God's Church; but all authentic ways must retain the indispensable structure apart from which the drama falls into the merest clowning. We must be open to the vast variety of possibilities of celebrating the Church's joy; but we must also guard against those possibilities that may fundamentally destroy the Church's lifeblood.

So the Creed affirms belief in the Church as having three marks or qualities: (1) it is One, (2) it is Catholic, and (3) it is Apostolic. What do such notions mean in our time?

That the Church is One is crucially important. Beyond all the millions of churches gathered and locally established and beyond all the tragic divisions in Christianity, the True Church must be One. It can no more be two or a dozen or a myriad than can God so be. As God can manifest himself in various modes and as the

Church may worship God in many ways, each right in its way, so can the Church be constantly renewed by the power of the Spirit of God; yet she can never be other than One, as God is One, as Truth is One, as Love is One. We must look beyond the sad schisms of the Church to see its fundamental unity. That is by no means to say that the differences between churches do not matter. To have false ideas about the nature or structure of the human body can lead to unpleasant, even disastrous consequences. So with the Church: false understandings of it can lead to futile or even disastrous results. Nevertheless, as there is one natural structure of the human body, so there is only One Church, which God is gathering and developing in his own way beyond all our human follies and despite all human arrogance and stupidity.

The Creed also affirms a belief in the Church as Catholic. What does it mean to talk of the Church as *Catholic?* The word *katholikos* means primarily "universal" or "general." In now archaic English usage one talked of a catholic cure, meaning a panacea, a remedy for all diseases, or of a catholic fish, a fish not peculiar to one region but found in all waters. The use of that adjective in connection with the Christian Church occurs very early, being found in a letter to the Church of Smyrna by Ignatius of Antioch, who was martyred in Rome in 107, only about a generation after the martyrdoms of Peter and Paul.

As applied to the Church the word *Catholic* has several different uses. From early times it was used to specify the universal Church contradistinguished from local churches at Ephesus, Antioch, and elsewhere, and it is in this sense that it is applied to the faith of the whole Church, contradistinguished from local deviations and idiosyncracies. In the fifth century Vincent of Lérins provided a guide, later known as the Vincentian Canon, for determining what is authentic Catholic doctrine. First, Holy Scripture is the basis; but in its interpretation the Church must distinguish true traditions from false, and here the test is threefold and in this order: "what has been believed everywhere, always, and by all" (*quod ubique, quod semper, quod ab omnibus creditum est*). This test, despite all the difficulties it raises, still provides a useful criterion. In modern practice, the Roman Church has come to apply the designation "Catholic" to itself exclusively; Anglicans generally apply it to themselves, to the Eastern Church, and to the

Roman Church as together representing the undivided Church of the early centuries. Some other Churches use it occasionally to signify their claim to historic continuity of faith and practice in contradistinction to those Protestant sects who claim to appeal to the Bible only.

The importance of the term *Catholic* in the Creed lies in its calling attention to the need to distinguish authentic Christian faith both from bogus and from desiccated versions of it. We should notice that "Catholic" is not a quality that a Church simply has or has not as a man might be said to be solvent or bankrupt. It is, rather, a quality one may have in fulness or in a more or less diminished degree, as a musician might talk of a perfect tonality as opposed to both very close approximations and deplorably off-key attempts.

The belief professed in the Creed is in the Church not only as One and Catholic but also as Apostolic. To say that the Church is Apostolic is not to say that it adheres only to doctrines specifically taught by the twelve apostles or other teachers and leaders in the Church of the first century. Saying that would exclude doctrines such as the Trinity, generally associated with the most firmly established traditions of the Church, as it would exclude also some of the most venerated Christian practices. What we affirm is, rather, that the faith and practice of the Church so conforms to the faith and practice of the Church in apostolic times that we can claim that the life that is flowing in us today is the same stream of life that flowed in the Church in apostolic times, having its source in the divine energy of the Holy Spirit. Possession of the historic episcopate has been widely taken to be an assurance of the continuity of the Church from the earliest times down to the present; hence the importance of the episcopate in ecclesial theory today. It does not by any means necessarily imply a monarchical or jurisdictional understanding of the nature of the episcopate, which is a separate concept.

The individual Christian, in the course of his or her pilgrimage, may receive more support from the Church in some cases than in others; always, however, he or she must recognize the Church as Mother of all faithful Christians. That is why corruption in the Church, especially in an unworthy bishop, brings such extreme sadness to the most loving Christian hearts. Yet the mature Christian, he or she who has entered into the highest level of awareness of what the Church is, sees beyond all such pollution of the Church Militant here on earth to the mystical union that we have with all those who have gone before us in the life beyond. These include not only the men and women, some of them our own close friends and relatives, who are on their way to fulfilment of Christ's promise for them, but also others, including some of our own kith and kin, who have already attained that glorious destiny. Such sensitive Christians rejoice daily in the knowledge that they are in full mystical communion with those who have gone beyond the veil of death yet are in one way or another present with us, especially as we gather together for the Holy Eucharist. The Church on earth prays *for* them as well as for ourselves here on earth, for they need our prayers and we who love them most earnestly desire to offer these prayers for their help; but where the Church believes they have already attained the destiny promised by Christ, we pray *to* them that *we* may be helped by their prayers. In this way Christians not only sustain brothers and sisters who are with us in this present life and are sustained by them; we also sustain and are sustained by the multitudes who have gone before us into further life beyond the veil of death, where they grow more fully into the stature that is our Christian hope.

We can radiantly perceive Paul's mystical conception of the Church as the Body of Christ, with our Lord himself as the Head, in the fellowship we have at every celebration of the Holy Eucharist. Here the priest joins the faithful physically present with the vast company of invisible worshippers, the angels and archangels, all the "heavenly hosts," and not least our own departed friends, who are not less present, being at another stage of the pilgrimage to glory.

Of all notions that stultify our minds and choke our hearts in our apprehension of the significance of the Church, none is more pernicious than the notion that the Church is limited to those who happen to be physically present with us at Sunday worship or at the potluck suppers and parish picnics. We can know little of the inner meaning of the Church till we see beyond that all-too-finite little group to the vast company beyond who are struggling with us for the coming of the kingdom of God and farther still to the unseen multitudes beyond the veil of death who are worshipping with us in joy.

The spiritual hazard faced in all churchgoing and in even the noblest kinds of worship has been well expressed by George Mac-Donald: "There is nothing more deadening to the divine than a habitual dealing in the outsides of holy things." These words should be engraved on the hearts of all churchpeople and especially on those of the clergy, who are in a special way exposed to the danger. We need constantly to be reminded that we are worshipping God through humble veils and that if we fail to penetrate them we shall end by worshipping stone and wood rather than the living God that they enshrine. "It is the Spirit that quickeneth" (John 6:63, KJV).

O God, who biddest us dwell with one mind in thine house: Of thy mercy put away from us all that causeth us to differ, that through thy bountiful goodness we may keep the unity of the Spirit in the bond of peace; through Jesus Christ our Lord.

—Edward Bouverie Pusey
(nineteenth century)

───── CHAPTER XIV ─────

One Baptism

I acknowledge one Baptism for the remission of sins

BAPTISM is one of two fundamental sacraments in the Christian Church. It is closely connected with the other, the sacrament of Holy Communion, which perpetually renews and sustains that which Baptism irrevocably accomplishes. For various reasons, Baptism has become a difficult and controversial question among theologians today. Nevertheless, its fundamental nature and purpose can be simply stated.

The primary function of Baptism is to admit a person into the Church. We may best think of it in connection with the notion of the Church as the Body of Christ, which we considered in the previous chapter. Through Baptism one is incorporated (embodied) into the Church. We may then think of the baptized person as a cell in that mystical Body, entry into which signifies a new birth, a regeneration. The life of the Body of Christ is to be thought of as flowing through and spiritually vitalizing that which has been incorporated into it. The baptized person may also be said to share mystically in the death and resurrection of Christ and to be anointed as partaking of Christ's holy character. Above all, Baptism imprints a new and indelible character on him or her who receives it.

Though various additional ritual acts and ceremonies may be used in administering Baptism, having come down to us from ancient or medieval practice, two are generally recognized throughout the Christian Church as indispensable. These are (1) water and (2) the use of the threefold name of God: Father, Son, and Holy Spirit. Two methods of administering the water have been in use from early times, and both are mentioned in the *Didache*, a manual of Christian practice which, though its date is disputed, is an early and very important witness. These methods are (1) triple immersion of the person in water, the method still used in the Greek Church, each immersion accompanied by the naming of one of the three Persons of the Trinity, and (2) affusion, the pouring of water on the head, the method generally used in the Roman Catholic, Lutheran, Anglican, and Reformed Church traditions.

Theologians today habitually complain of the indubitable fact that most people understand this sacrament too crudely. We are all too much disposed to look at the outside of Christian teaching and practice and too little at its inner significance; in the case of Baptism, however, this general tendency is particularly notable and lamentably injurious to our understanding of the inner meaning of everything else in our practice and tradition. The failure to see behind externals into the mystical significance of Baptism is by no means confined to people in the contemporary age. In the fourth century, Gregory of Nyssa, about the time of the formulation of the Creed we are examining (which, by the way, he warmly supported), complained of that same thing, remarking that although "they have been instructed that it is prayer and the invocation of heavenly grace, and water, and faith, by which the mystery of regeneration is accomplished, they still remain incredulous and have an eye only for the outward and visible, as if that which is operated corporeally did not concur with the fulfilment of God's promises." Ambrose, his contemporary in the West, also alludes to the tendency to suppose that the grace resides in the water when in fact, he insists, if there be "any grace in the water, it is not from the nature of the water, but from the presence of the Holy Spirit." The early Fathers commonly insist that the water has no virtue in itself: by itself it is just a common element; it becomes a vehicle for grace only when joined to the Church's faith in the Cross of Christ.

Popular misunderstanding of Baptism is reflected in the widespread notion that what distinguishes Baptists from the other Christian churches is their insistence on the total immersion of adult candidates for the sacrament. In fact, the difference is much more profound. In the first place, though the practice of infant baptism is general in all the churches already mentioned, all of them occasionally baptize adults as need arises. In the second place, as already noted, the Greeks baptize infants by immersion, though this is not customary among the other churches mentioned. What distinguishes Baptist belief and practice from the belief and practice of these other traditions is a radically different understanding of the nature not only of the sacrament but also of the Church. On the Baptist view, Baptism is indeed an entry into the Church, but each congregation of believers is conceived as a separate entity, and each individual is to be admitted only when he or she can personally attest his or her belief in Christ and personally make the undertakings necessary for a Christian life, which means the candidate must be a grown man or woman. The concept of mystical incorporation into the Body of Christ in infancy is absent.

While there is no specific allusion in the New Testament to children having been baptized, there are references to the baptism of entire households. Although this might not be sufficient scriptural warrant in the eyes of some, there are weighty reasons for believing that, while of course adult baptism would be very frequent at first, since so many adults were converted to the Christian Way, those who had children would have their children baptized with the rest of the household. At any rate, the witness of the earliest Fathers is unanimous that infant baptism was normal practice. Irenaeus, for example, who develops a very thorough doctrine of Baptism, is explicit on the point. Moreover, Baptism was interpreted as closely associated with the old rite of circumcision. It was a "spiritual" circumcision. The rule that the baptized and the unbaptized were not allowed to eat at the same table applied to both parents and children, clearly implying that Christian children were baptized, since otherwise they could not have lived under the same roof with their parents.

The scriptural warrant for Baptism has sometimes been taken to be the injunction of the Risen Christ to the disciples (Matt. 28:19), in which he commands them to go forth to teach all nations, baptizing them. The ground for Christian Baptism lies, rather, in the acceptance by Jesus himself of baptism by John the

Baptist. Jesus provides further support in remarks such as that no man can enter into the kingdom of God unless he be "born of water and of the Spirit" (John 3:5). At any rate, the emphasis on baptism in the practice of the apostles as recounted in Acts leaves us in no doubt at all that baptism was accounted essential for entrance into the Church. With rare exceptions, all Christian bodies today insist on baptism as a condition of entry. The most notable exceptions are the Quakers and the Salvation Army.

Baptism was believed from early times to bring about forgiveness of sins; hence the reference to this in the Creed. Even infants needed this, because of inheritance from their parents of the common sinfulness of the entire human race. The primary condition of the efficacy of Baptism, apart from the ritual words and action, is faith. The infant cannot make a profession of faith personally; but his or her parents or sponsors make it in his or her place and in the name of the whole Church. Again we see the mystical basis of the entire proceeding. The little child, in all his or her helplessness, is borne up by the Church into which he or she is incorporated. Parents or other sponsors undertake to bring the child up in a Christian atmosphere so that, as he or she grows up, the faith of the Church may be appropriated by the child and become his or her own.

Baptism provides the infant with spiritual opportunity. As we must all make what we can of our birth, so we must make what we can of our rebirth into the Church. Baptism is inseparably connected with faith. Faith is the gift of the Spirit, as the New Testament insists, and it is only through faith that we continue to receive the Spirit. Baptism initiates us into a mutual relation between the Holy Spirit and faith. The Holy Spirit acts creatively upon us, but we must so walk in faith that we respond to God and receive his grace.

The Creed speaks of *one* Baptism because the baptism of the individual presupposes the one Baptism common to Christ and his Church. Once again we encounter a mystical understanding of the whole concept. The individual takes his or her place in the Body of Christ in which Christ acts and rules and gives the Communion of his Body and Blood, for, as we saw at the outset, Baptism and Communion are intimately and inseparably bound together.

Historically associated with Baptism is the rite of Confirmation. Although this rite goes back to early times, it has been variously administered and understood. According to Catholic tradition it also confers a "character" on the recipient. It seems that in early times it was really a part of the sacrament of Baptism itself. By the fourth century, however, it had become a separate rite, conferred either by an anointing or a laying-on of hands. No doubt the increase in numbers had by then made it difficult or impossible for bishops to take personal interest in all candidates for Baptism, as had been possible in earlier times, so that responsibility was delegated to parish and other priests. In the East the primitive practice of associating Confirmation directly with Baptism was retained: the Bishop consecrated the oil, which was then conveyed to the parish or other priest so that he could perform the rite. As soon as the infant received the anointing, Communion was administered to him or her. This has remained substantially the practice in the Eastern Church today. In the West, however, the Bishop remained the regular minister of Confirmation, which was therefore often deferred for a long time, awaiting his convenience; but the ideal of conferring the two rites together, as in the East, was never entirely lost, and some attempts have been made in recent times to bring them together in practice.

The Anglican Communion and others have used Confirmation as an opportunity for general instruction in Christian faith and practice; hence the custom of preparing candidates by a series of classes. Much controversy among theologians has arisen over the precise nature of Confirmation, but two points seem clear: (1) nothing should be done to suggest that Baptism without Confirmation is in any way incomplete, and (2) Confirmation provides a useful opportunity for young people to take for themselves the vows undertaken for them at their baptism in the presence of a congregation of the faithful People of God, as well as to submit themselves to the influence of the Spirit and to resolve, as best they can, to be good soldiers of Christ.

So much emphasis has been placed on the absolute necessity of baptism for Christians that it has been widely held in the history of the Church to be completely indispensable for salvation. Augustine, however, provided for exceptional cases, as, for instance, where a person earnestly desires baptism but is prevented by circumstances from receiving it. Yet so central to Christian belief and tradition is Baptism that most Christians from the earliest times have accounted it the one sacramental act that marks Christians off from other people. Anyone who is truly convinced of the realities to which Christian teaching points will seek to be joined to the Church through this sacrament (*mystērion*), setting him or her apart from the world and opening up the other great sacrament of Holy Communion.

How are we to relate all that to modern thought? There is no doubt at all that the concept of Baptism emerged in a world in which the value and importance of the individual was not so generally appreciated as it is today. In the ancient and medieval world people thought more in terms of societies and groups and of the individual's participation in them. The development of the basic theory of Baptism reflects that outlook.

What of the strong individualist today who feels ill at ease with the modes of thought that prevailed when baptism was developed? Is there no room for "loners" in the Christian Way? One thinks, for example, of one of the greatest Christian geniuses of the century, if not in all the long history of the Church: Simone Weil (1909–43). Jewish by birth, Catholic by temper and conviction, this great Frenchwoman steadfastly declined to receive Baptism. A mystic of extraordinary compassion and sensitivity of heart, who devoted herself to the welfare of humanity to the point of virtually starving herself to an early death, she had also an exceptionally brilliant mind. (She was first in the competitive examination for the Ecole Normale Supérieure, for example, beating Simone de Beauvoir and, at twenty-one, emerging from that prestigious institution as a fully qualified teacher of philosophy in France.) Her writings exhibit extraordinarily profound insight into what the Christian Way entails. Can one dare to call such a person a non-Christian because she chose to die without receiving Baptism?

Yet Baptism is a concept inseparable from that of the Church, from which few Christians, even among the greatest individualists, ever seek to be separate, for they feel the need to belong to it if only to practice that humility that was in Christ Jesus our Lord. Many among them also feel they need the strengthening that comes from the life that flows through the Church by the Spirit of God and also feel no less the duty and the wish to be channels of grace to the rest of the Church. So, although the complete "loner" is not unthinkable among Christians, he or she is rare indeed. Such a path is exceptionally difficult and fraught with peril, not least the peril of pride leading to false pretensions to spiritual attainment and false claims to knowledge of divine things. The vast majority of even the most spiritually advanced men and women, even the great mystics who have gone beyond dependence on the Church for their spiritual survival, know well (often better than others) that as human beings we must participate in the community that is the People of God, the Household of Faith, not only to take but to give. Baptism remains the door through which we are introduced to the life of faith in Christ.

The tragic divisions among Christians remain in our time, ecumenical projects notwithstanding. They separate Christians not only at the altar in the central focus of worship, the Eucharist, but in the entire style of Christian life. Baptism, however, does provide one great unifying link, binding together Christians of every kind. For, generally speaking, despite the controversies that still rage about Faith and Order, Baptism is almost universally accepted among all Christian bodies irrespective of the aegis under which it is administered. One Church may customarily wish persons who have been already baptized in another Church to be conditionally baptized under the formula: "If you are not already baptized, I baptize you. . . ." In principle, however, Baptism is unique in having that universal recognition among Christians of all sorts. It is the hallmark of a Christian, attesting that, however nominal the allegiance, he or she has been marked out in love and belongs forever to Christ.

O Lord God Almighty, who hast commanded thy servants to be born again of water and the Holy Spirit; preserve in them the holy Baptism which they have received, and be pleased to perfect it to the hallowing of thy Name; that thy grace may ever increase upon them, and that what they have already received by thy gift they may guard by integrity of life; through Jesus Christ our Lord.

—Gallican Sacramentary

CHAPTER XV

The Life of the World To Come

And I look for the Resurrection of the dead,
And the Life of the world to come

"GOOD Master," said the rich man to Jesus, "what must I do to inherit eternal life?" (Mark 10:17; cf. Matt. 19:16; Luke 10:25, 18:18). In the milieu in which Jesus moved, the question was a much less surprising one than it might be in contemporary society, for the Christian Way emerged in a climate of thought in which people were seeking personal salvation. To many the thought of extinction was abhorrent, and they wanted to know how to avoid it and acquire instead the power to attain endless (*aiōnios*) life. Today some affect to view as selfish such a preoccupation with one's personal attainment of everlasting life. Yet it is at the very heart of all seeking after God. How can I expect to be able to help others in their spiritual pilgrimage if I do not even know where I am going myself? The problem of one's personal destiny is an existential one, inseparable from Christian faith. Profound interest in it is presupposed both in the New Testament itself and in all early Christian tradition.

We have seen that Paul holds out the promise of resurrection for all Christians on the ground that Christ has risen. The classical Hebrew tradition had held out no hope of a joyous afterlife. The deceased was "gathered to the fathers" or went down to a vague abode of the dead (*sheol*), somewhat like the underworld (*hades*) that was its counterpart in the thought of the Greeks in the time of Homer. In later Jewish thought, however, under foreign influence, some groups, such as the Pharisees, took seriously the possibility of some sort of resurrection. The concept of the soul as intrinsically immortal, which was widespread in the Hellenic world under various forms and had Plato's blessing, was alien to the Hebrew tradition. The concept of reincarnation, which was widespread in the Hellenic world in both primitive and developed ethical forms, was also a stranger to classic Hebrew thought. Such traces of it as may be detected in Jewish thought by the time of Christ seem to be due to foreign influence.

What, then, can we say of Christian thought about afterlife in New Testament times? Above all, it was vague and confused. For this we know an excellent reason. As we have already noted in connection with the Christian belief in the Second Coming, the disciples and other early followers of the Christian Way expected the end to come very soon. Though the exact time was not revealed, they assumed that it would not be far off. Could we have asked any group of Christians in the first century when they expected it, they would have said that it would be soon, and no doubt some would have pointed out that it might well be the next day: the sooner the better. "Come, Lord Jesus" (Rev. 22:20) represented a standard sentiment among them. They believed they were in a new age, an interim period that would be of short duration. Because of this belief, they were naturally not disposed to speculate about the nature of their destiny: they knew it would be "with the Lord," and that was all that mattered. The possibility of an "intermediate state," moreover, which was to play an increasingly large part in the thought of Christians from the second century onwards, was not less naturally absent from their thoughts. Those who died before the Second Coming were accounted "asleep in Christ" and that is indeed a characteristic type of epitaph in the catacombs. So soon was the Second Coming expected that younger people might well hope to see their elders awakened by the sound of it and to unite with them in joy. In such circumstances one does not engage in metaphysical speculations about the details of the life to come. Assured of the Lord's triumph and of his coming reign of justice and love, what more need one ask?

As time went on, however, and the Day of Judgment did not

come, the hope, though it continued, took a different form. The Day was no longer such an imminent expectation. By this time, of course, various utterances had accumulated about the Christian hope, reflecting presuppositions about the life to come that had been often if not generally acquired accidentally and unconsciously, depending among other things on the background of the Christians in question. The result was an extraordinary confusion in early Christian doctrine on the life to come, a confusion whose germs are already to be found in the New Testament. Paul cannot say precisely what the "glorified body" will be; he is sure only that the flesh-and-blood body of our present state cannot share in the kingdom of God (I Cor. 15:50), for the qualities of the glorious body are the negation of the present one. This is an admirable way for Paul to express two important concepts: (1) a body (soma) of some sort is essential; it need not be a fleshy one (sarx) but could be far better; and (2) whatever body we are to have must be suitable for "heaven," which means it must be "glorious," that is, of greater luminosity. Paul follows a Jewish tradition in conceptualizing a plurality of heavens. In Hebrew the word is plural: shamāyim. So Paul could talk of having been carried up into the third heaven (II Cor. 12:2) in the course of an ecstatic experience of some kind.

The third heaven was sometimes identified with Paradise, the place where, according to Luke's account, Jesus promises the repentant thief they will be together "today." Paradise was only one of the many aspects of the New Testament conception of life after death. It might even represent an intermediate state. The notion of an intermediate state, such as was much later developed in Christian thought as a purificatory process (purgatory), arose, as we have seen, only after the early Christian hope of an imminent Second Coming had receded; nevertheless, the notion of prayers for the dead, which implies an intermediate state of some kind, can be found in Judaism a century or more before the Christian era (II Macc. 12:42f.). "Paradise" comes from an old Persian word meaning a large park with trees and streams such as one would expect in the grounds of a great palace. It is used in this general sense three times in the Hebrew Bible (Neh. 2:8; Song of Sol. 4:13; Eccles. 2:5). Closely associated with the Garden of Eden, it became naturally the way of expressing, in later pre-

Christian Judaism, the destination of the righteous. It is sometimes represented as an interim abode between death and the final
judgment.

The earliest Christian teaching is certainly clear that while
the lot of the righteous after death is supremely desirable, the lot
of the unrighteous is correspondingly undesirable. The precise
nature of the destiny of the wicked, however, is as unclear as is
that of the righteous. A notion found in the New Testament expresses it in terms of Gehenna, which refers to a particular geo-
graphical location dividing the old Jerusalem (Zion) from the hills
to the south and west: the modern Wadi er Rababi. For various
reasons the place was deemed an accursed dump. It became, therefore, a natural symbol for the place no one would want to go, and
it acquired a secondary connotation as a general incinerator and
trash heap for rubbish. So in the New Testament it is a natural
way of expressing the lot of the wicked after death. The Bible is not
at all clear, however, about what precisely is the fate of these unrighteous men and women. One might argue for several possibilities: that they lie stinking and rotting; that they are burned
up; that they burn forever; or that they are annihilated. All that is
clear is that they are throw-outs and so go to the trash bin. Both
the original indefiniteness and the original significance are somewhat curiously reflected in the modern vulgar and abusive phrase
"go to hell," which has of course no developed theological allusion
but means, rather, "get out of the stream of life and into the
rubbish heap where you belong," or something of that sort.

When Christianity spread to the Gentile world and the imminent expectation of the Second Coming had waned, Christian
thought was left with not only a wide variety of options about the
expectations for both the wicked and the righteous, both the saved
and the damned, but also a conglomeration of various ideas imper-
fectly welded together: a mess of category confusions. These confusions have persisted to this day, so that if you were to run an
opinion poll, using for the sampling a carefully selected repre-
sentation of intelligent and thoughtful Christians, you would get
an astoundingly confused set of answers about what they took to
be the standard or orthodox understanding of the destiny of men
and women after death.

Let us suppose that Aunt Bessie has died last week. What

would they say of her present status and expectation, assuming she had been a good Christian? Some would say she was asleep in Christ, awaiting the resurrection in a disembodied state; there was no point in praying for her, since her final destiny had already been assured, and it was only a matter of waiting for it to be realized. Others would say she had gone to "heaven" at once and received a "resurrection body" but presumably only a temporary one, since she would get a permanent one at the General Resurrection on the Day of Judgment. Some might even say that she was in heaven but would not have a body and would not need one till the Day of Judgment. Still others would say she was probably in purgatory and would much benefit from our prayers, but whether she needed a body in purgatory would not be clear. Only the simplistic would envision heaven as a place with pearly gates and streets of gold and purgatory as a seven-storeyed mountain; but the others would rightly be disinclined to specify anything about heaven except that it would be a state of bliss and that the bliss would derive from closeness to God. With Whittier they might say:

> I know not where His islands lift
> Their fronded palms in air;
> I only know I cannot drift
> Beyond His love and care.

But what if Aunt Bessie had been a monstrously wicked woman and a sworn enemy of Christ? Some might say she would be already in hell, a place or state of everlasting torment. If you asked whether God might not be merciful enough to let her off with extinction rather than impose such a horrific sentence of everlasting punishment, they might possibly say that since the souls of men and women are immortal they must go somewhere; they cannot die. Others would question this and suggest that only those who are redeemed by Christ can hope for life everlasting; the unredeemed would just die as do the lower animals. (These questioners would have much support in Paul.) Some might even ask why the lower animals should not be eligible, at least in some measure, for the bliss of the redeemed. (These would have scant support in Christian tradition, which has never had much to say on such matters.) Then since the predictions about the Second Coming seem to imply that both the good and the evil are to get back their bodies, some thoughtful people in the sampling group would ask what sort of bodies the wicked would have and what they would do with them in hell; also what they would have done without them if, as is believed by some, they would have been already there, possibly for millions of years before the Last Day.

Such answers, though they do not exhaust all the difficulties or exhibit all the confusions, give some notion of the muddle in which traditional Christian theory about what is sometimes called "Last Things" now stands and to a great extent already stood by the time the Nicene Creed was formulated in the fourth century. Wisely, therefore, the Nicene Fathers restricted their affirmation of belief concerning questions of this kind to two points: (1) there is to be a resurrection of the body and (2) there is future life, life in the world to come.

For, by the time the Creed was formulated, Christian thought had been exposed to many sophisticated speculations on the subject of immortality and resurrection. In sharp contrast to Paul, whose mind was cast in a Hebrew mold, Origen, for example, held that the soul had preexisted and was by its nature immortal, a view that he embedded in his unusual and complex theory of salvation over successive ages to come, that would see, before the end of that immensely long process, the salvation of everybody, including even Satan himself. Though the subject, because of textual difficulties, is controversial among scholars, I think there is good reason for believing that Origen taught a reincarnational doctrine of some sort.

Such reincarnational doctrines were by no means condemned out of hand in the early Church; they were too much part of the general intellectual climate of the Mediterranean world of the time. Justin Martyr, in his *Dialogue with Trypho*, discusses Trypho's primitivistic type of reincarnationist view, which entertained the possibility of rebirth into the body of a beast, and he discountenanced that particular form of reincarnationism; but that he and many others took reincarnation in its more developed and moral form as a viable option for Christian thought is highly probable. All that concerns us here is that innumerable options were available, since neither the New Testament nor later Christian tradition gave any specific directions on the nature of "the life

of the world to come," beyond saying that for the righteous it
would be the unspeakable bliss of "seeing" God and living in his
presence and, for the wicked, of being excluded from that inde-
scribably happy prospect.

The sharp distinction that modern scholars such as Oscar
Cullmann have made between theories of immortality and theories
of resurrection is useful, but it should not be overestimated. For
while the notion that the soul is intrinsically imperishable is more
typically Greek than Hebrew, Greek and other ideas so affected
late pre-Christian Jewish thought, even in Palestine itself, as to
diminish the sharpness of the distinction. More importantly, however, though some of the Athenians "burst out laughing" when
Paul spoke of the raising of Jesus Christ from the dead, the concept
of resurrection was not by any means alien to the thought of the
Hellenic world. Reincarnation is, after all, a form of resurrection
(both certainly imply reembodiment of some kind), and it was an
ancient belief that Plato's Socrates took seriously and that Plato
accepted as part of the ancient Pythagorean wisdom.

The educated Gentile world was more accustomed to the
concept of an intrinsically immortal soul than were the Hebrews.
When Christianity spread to the Gentile world this concept eventually gave rise to speculation about the fate of those who would
not attain everlasting life with God "in heaven." Since they could
not perish absolutely in the sense of being annihilated, they must
(such was the general feeling) go on existing in a misery as everlasting as the bliss of the redeemed. In popular imagination,
nourished by fiery preaching, hell became a constant terror. Elaborate supportive doctrines connected with it were developed, such as
that certain sins (called "mortal" because they "killed" the soul)
were so grave that if one died in such a state of sin, impenitently,
one was a sure candidate for eternal punishment. This view, which
prevailed in the medieval Church in the West, was carried over by
the Reformers. In popular preaching by the heirs of the Reformation the fear of hell was vigorously instilled into people's minds,
being standard pulpit pabulum on both sides of the Reformation
curtain till at least a century ago, and by no means unheard of
since. Awesome images of leering devils sadistically torturing their
victims with red-hot pokers and of the damned dancing everlastingly in unremitting agony in a suffocating, flaming furnace

frightened millions. The learned, while not entirely renouncing such a view, generally followed the great thirteenth-century schoolman Thomas Aquinas in insisting that the essence of hell is the sense of the eternal loss of God, the source of all good.

The pains of purgatory were also fearsomely depicted; but the thought of them was, besides being more intelligible, infinitely less horrific, if only because of their temporary duration. Even if they were to last whatever would be the equivalent in purgatorial time of a million years, they would come to an end and be exchanged for the everlasting bliss of heaven. Moreover, one would have all along the blessed assurance that one was on the way to everlasting beatitude, not to everlasting damnation.

The concept of purgatory was generally abandoned by the heirs of the Reformation, leaving them with the stark alternative of heaven or hell. In the thought of many, Aunt Bessie, when she died, must go straight to one or the other and so achieve immediately on death her everlasting destiny. Some thought of it as "eternal," that is, beyond time itself, while others thought of it as of infinite duration in time.

In the nineteenth century, largely through the influence of the English Tractarians, the concept of purgatory was revived but drastically revised: it was seen as a place more of cleansing and growth than of punishment, reformatory rather than penitentiary. This revised understanding of the nature of purgatory as a place of continuing education and growth, together with the extremely muddled state of the Christian tradition about the future life and the philosophical and scientific puzzles attending the muddle, cannot but arouse in thinking Christians a deep sense of the need to restate the Christian concept of the future life.

What the Nicene Creed does is above all to deny the widespread view (common in people insensitive to spiritual realities) that the silence of the grave is all that lies beyond death. On this view man's only consolation is that, as Frederick the Great is said to have remarked, when looking at the royal tombs at Potsdam: *alors je serai sans souci,* "then I shall be untroubled." Against this common sense of the finality of death, the Christian who affirms his or her faith in the words of the Nicene Creed is asserting that, to the contrary, he or she sees beyond death to a fuller life in a finer embodiment. Beyond that the Creed does not go. Many

Christians have been inclined to leave the details of the future life to their Saviour rather than to pretend to know what seems to be unknowable. Nevertheless, our faith in Christ *implies*, besides much else, the vision of ongoing life and the enrichment of the quality of our being that an increasing knowledge of the love of God must bring.

We are free to make our own speculations about how it may work. We can choose from among various possibilities the one that seems the best expression of what the fuller presence of God will mean: whether it will entail more rest than work or more work than rest, for example. Whatever it will be, it cannot be static; it must be dynamic, for life is by nature dynamic, and a fuller life must surely be even more dynamic than the present one in which we are embodied in flesh and trapped by the burdens of our psyche. To be closer to God means to have an enhanced freedom, for service to God, as the old collect acknowledges, *is* to be free. We cannot expect less than the vision of the Deutero-Isaiah, that those who hope in the Lord "renew their strength, they put out wings like eagles. They run and do not grow weary, walk and never tire" (Isa. 40:31, JB).

Work, even in the best of causes, is tedious and frustrating when our energies flag and we feel burned out and unfitted for the task. With the body of greater luminosity that we are promised (the "glorified" body) our efficiency will be enhanced and our energies better deployed. At the same time, most of us know (and this is what the doctrine of an intermediate state has always recognized) that, despite all that Christ has done for us to make possible our attainment of the life of the world to come, we are not yet ready to enjoy the most perfect closeness with God that we are capable of attaining. Our ears are not yet attuned to the finest of the heavenly music. We need more preparation, more opportunity to appropriate the gifts our Saviour Christ has laid aside for us. In our Lord's own words, there are many mansions in heaven. His promise is to go ahead of us "to prepare a place" for us. In that picturesque language we catch a glimpse of the nature of our glorious destiny and how it is to unfold in the life of the world to come.

The Creed says nothing specifically about the question that is foremost in the minds of all who have known the joy of walking through life in the company of loved ones who have gone before them across the veil: will they meet them again on another shore? Certainly all Christian tradition supports the view that the fuller life to come implies such a recognition of and meeting with those friends who have meant so much to us in the present life. What could it mean to talk of a fuller life in Christ for me if it did not encompass the renewal in some form or other of the deepest relationships I have known in my current pilgrimage? What growth in love would it be that permanently excluded what I have known of these relationships and treated them as if they had never been? Through them more than in any other way I have known the presence of God. They have been superlatively holy relationships. Surely if my friends and I are to be "in Christ," we cannot be everlastingly separated?

The belief that we shall meet our friends beyond the veil of death is an ancient one known to sages before the time of Christ and among those whose lives have been cast apart from the Christian heritage. "And perhaps," writes Seneca, "if only the tale told by the wise men be true, and there is a place to welcome us, then he whom we think we have lost has only been sent on ahead." If those we call pagans could cherish such a hope, surely it cannot be excluded from our vision of the "life of the world to come"?

The clue lies in the penultimate phrase of the Creed: the resurrection of the dead. Through our reembodiment recognition is made possible. We do not know when or where or how we shall meet or what precisely will be the nature of such a relationship in the life beyond; it is enough to know it will be better than ever since it will be more fully "in Christ." And yet in those hallowed moments when we can catch a glimpse of the glory of that other side of the veil, the presence of our loved ones draws nearer and the light they bear gives us, if only for a fleeting moment, an awareness of the joy of the meeting that lies in store for us, which the time of waiting can but enhance.

We began our study of the joy of the Nicene Creed with the individual in his or her loneliness engaging in the act of faith: I believe! We have considered difficulties and we have viewed them in the light of modern knowledge that the Nicene Fathers were not privileged to possess. We have seen the Creed in a light that should strengthen our Christian hope.

Meanwhile, I am glad, with John Henry Newman, if the

"kindly light" should enable me to say "one step enough for me"
and to carry me on through all loneliness and darkness until

> the night is gone
> And with the morn those angel faces smile
> Which I have loved long since, and lost awhile.

After all, if I am to see the fullness of the light of Christ, how can
it fail to illumine for me the presence of those helpers, known and
unknown, seen and unseen, who have watched over me all
through my life and have shown me how to turn the once flicker-
ing candle of my faith into a flaming torch?

> MAY the holy angels of God come forth to meet him [her],
> and conduct him [her] into the heavenly city,
> Jerusalem. . . .

> MAY Christ receive thee, who hath called thee,
> and may the angels bear thee into Abraham's bosom. . . .
>
> —Rituale Romanum,
> Prayers for a departing soul

> AND we also bless thy holy name for all thy servants
> departed this life in thy faith and fear; beseeching thee to
> grant them continual growth in thy love and service. . . .
>
> —Book of Common Prayer
> (American, 1928)

Index

Abba, 11
Abraham, 3, 5, 68
Acts, 39
Adoptianists, 57
Adventists, 99
Agapē, 88, 111, 116
Alētheia, 116
Allegorization, medieval, 7, 116
Almightiness, 12f.
Ambrose, 127
Angels, 11, 23f., 87, 89
Anna, 59
Annihilation, 52, 137
Antioch, 122
Apeiron, to, 19
Aphrodite, 9
Apostles' Creed, 75
Aquinas. *See* Thomas Aquinas
Arianism, 42
Aristotle, 2, 46, 58n., 67
Arius, 41f.
Ascension, 86, 90ff.
Astral body. *See* Body of Light
Athos, Mount, 119
Augustine, 20, 44, 55, 59f., 111, 119ff., 130
Avatar, 33f.

Baptism: Baptists' view of, 127f.; of Jesus, 40; spiritual affinity of sponsors at, 2; theology of, 126ff.
Barth, Karl, 20, 64, 68
Beauvoir, Simone de, 131
Being of Light, 94. *See also* Body of Light

Belief, 1ff.
Believing that/in, 1ff.
Betullah, 65
Bezaleel, 108
"Big bang" theory, 22
Biology, 14, 61ff.
Body, complexity of human, 50, 83f.
Body of Light, 85, 88, 92
Body of Christ, 78, 119ff., 124, 126, 128f.
Bonnat, Léon, 87
Brain, 50
Brown, Lesley, 62
Burial, 77

Cadbury, H. J., 36
Calvin, John, 20, 92, 121
Cappadocians, 111
Carthusians, motto of the, 77
Catacombs, 134
Cave, allegory of the, 25
Chaldean liturgy, 27
Charlemagne, 110
Chateaubriand, 96
Chesterton, G. K., 53
China, 32, 95
Chromosomes, 62
Church, 88, 118ff.; and Holy Spirit, 112; and State, 76
Circumcision and Baptism, 128
City of God, 76
Claes, Daniel, 61
Cloning, 62f.
Coleridge, S. T., 34
Confucius, 53

145